IN THE STEAD OF CHRIST:

The Relation of the Celebration of
the Lord's Supper to the
Office of the Holy Ministry

BY KENT A. HEIMBIGNER

✦ REPRISTINATION PRESS ✦

First Edition: April, 1998
Second Printing: April, 2011

REPRISTINATION PRESS
P.O. Box 173
Bynum, Texas 76631

ISBN 1-891469-24-X

TABLE OF CONTENTS

I.N.I.

There are a few people whom I cannot fail to thank for their assistance in the production of this work, which is a revision of my S.T.M. Thesis. First and foremost, I want to publicly thank my wife, Denise. She was my "word-perfect" before I got a similarly-named computer program. She has supported and encouraged me in my pastoral ministry, in my scholarly endeavors, and quite simply as my best friend. She has sacrificed her time with me and offered the insights of her formidable intellect in proofreading. When necessary, she has proven herself a faithful guardian of my humility, and she has always proven herself a faithful mother to our four children. When I wondered if there were any more daughters of Sarah (1 Peter 3:3-6), by the grace of God I found one. I would have to write another book in order to adequately express my gratitude to her, and for her. God grant me even to approach being a great a gift to her as she is to me.

Rev. Dr. Norman Nagel was my Thesis advisor, but that does not even begin to say what needs to be said. For whatever ability I have to think theologically, to write confessionally, and to properly distinguish between Law and Gospel, his teaching in large part is responsible. He would shame me for having recourse to anything but the words, but I cannot help but notice how his life bears witness to the doctrine he teaches, confesses, and proclaims. Thanks be to God for the gift of a man who has nothing to talk about other than the gifts that are ours in Christ Jesus.

Rev. Dr. Charles Arand was my Thesis reader. I appreciate the helpful corrections he made in the rough drafts. He was one of my professors, but he always spoke to me as an equal, and I am grateful for him, both as a professor and a friend.

Thanks to Mom and Dad, Gary and Stella Heimbigner. They have supported my education with their prayers, their love, and none too few of their dollars. Further, I would like to thank the congregations of Grace Lutheran Church in Marlin, Texas and Charity Lutheran Church in Burleson, Texas, where I have served as Pastor. They have been supportive of my ongoing scholarly endeavors, and I am most thankful to have served my Lord in these congregations.

Most of all, all praise and glory and wisdom and thanks and honor and power and strength be to our God forever and ever, for indeed salvation belongs to Him, and to the Lamb. In every word that I write, God forgive me what is mine, and bless what is His, for the sake of the holy precious blood and the innocent suffering and death of Jesus Christ my Lord. Amen.

Rev. Kent A. Heimbigner
Burleson, Texas
Epiphany, 1998

S.D.G.

INTRODUCTION

Jesus took bread, gave thanks and broke it, and gave it to His disciples, saying, "Take and eat; this is my body."

Then He took the cup, gave thanks and offered it to them, saying, "Drink from it, all of you. This is my blood of the covenant, which is poured out for many for the forgiveness of sins. I tell you, I will not drink of this fruit of the vine from now on until that day when I drink it anew with you in My Father's kingdom."

(Matthew 26:26-29)[1]

The Lord gives His Supper through His apostles to His Church. The direction of the giving of this gift is particularly evident in St. Paul's words: "For I received from the Lord what I also passed on to you ..." (1 Cor. 11:23). Here also one finds the mandate of the Lord to repeat His Supper. "To the Church of God in Corinth, ... together with all those everywhere who call on the name of our Lord Jesus Christ," the apostle says "when you come together as a church," it is to eat the bread/body and to drink the wine/blood, and so to be given the forgiveness of sins (1 Cor. 1:2; 11:18). This truth is plainly confessed in Martin Luther's *Small Catechism*:

> What is the Sacrament of the Altar?
> It is the true body and blood of our Lord Jesus Christ under the bread and wine, for us Christians to eat and drink, instituted by Christ Himself.[2]

Further:

> What is the benefit of such eating and drinking?
> That is shown us by these words, "Given and shed for you for the remission of sins"; namely, that in the Sacrament forgiveness of sins, life, and salvation are given us through these words. For where there is forgiveness of sins, there is also life and salvation.[3]

The questions addressed in this book concern the celebration of the Lord's Supper. Whom has the Lord entrusted with the celebration of His Supper? Has this celebration been given exclusively to those who have been placed into the Office of the Holy Ministry? How were the answers to these questions confessed in the liturgical writings of the early Church?

The liturgies of the early Church are the confessions of those who used them.[4] As they prayed, so they believed, and as they believed, so they prayed (*lex orandi-lex credendi*). The reason for examining the liturgies of the early Church is to examine the faith that the Church confessed. By so doing, one is better equipped to recognize that which has been handed down from the Lord through His apostles, and that which is an innovation added to the apostolic faith.

This book is written with the presupposition that the Holy Scriptures of the Old and New Testaments are the divinely-inspired, written Word of God.[5] This view is most consistent with an investigation of the liturgical writings of the early Church, as the earliest liturgies of the Church consist almost entirely of the words of Holy Scripture. Those who used these liturgies sought not to displace what they had received; rather, they confessed it as they had first received it.

This book does not undertake to prove from Scripture the doctrine of either the holy ministry or the Lord's Supper as they are articulated in the Lutheran Confessions; rather, it presupposes the correctness of that exposition. An exhaustive presentation of either of these doctrinal articles is not intended. This having been noted, it has nevertheless been found necessary to present scriptural evidence for certain aspects of these doctrines, particularly the doctrine of the holy ministry, in order to establish and lucidly to present an exposition of the relation of the Office of the Holy Ministry to the celebration of the Lord's Supper.

Therefore, in considering the relation of the Office of the Holy Ministry to the celebration of the Lord's Supper, this thesis is divided into three main parts. The first part contains the pertinent scriptural evidence. This part is further divided into four chapters. The first treats the Office of the Holy Ministry, the second addresses the Lord's Supper, and the third speaks to the relation of the Office of the Holy Ministry to the forgiveness of sins. Each of these three chapters begins with an examination of the Old Testament background material, followed by an examination of the pertinent New Testament data. The distinction between the Old and New Testament may at times seem strained. Often an author will make references to how the Old Testament goes into the New, and the placement of such information into either the Old Testament or the New Testament section of the chapter may at times appear arbitrary. The present author has sought in this way to present the information in a manner as orderly and easy to follow as possible, and where this goal is less than optimally accomplished, the indulgence of the reader is requested.

This first part of the thesis concludes with a chapter

which ties together the information presented in the three preceding chapters, incorporates some additional information, and presents the implications of this for the relation of the Office of the Holy Ministry to the celebration of the Lord's Supper.

The next step is to examine the liturgical data which are chronologically closest to our Lord's institution of both His Supper and His Holy Ministry. Unfortunately, there are no written texts which give a full account of a regular Sunday liturgy for roughly the first 300 years of the church's history. In order to compensate for the absence of such data, the author will draw on the writings of early church fathers and the texts of several church orders which provide insight into the liturgical confession and practice of the Church at that time. The last of the church orders that will be analyzed is the *Apostolic Constitutions*, which relied heavily upon the *Didache*, the *Didascalia*, and the *Apostolic Tradition* of Hippolytus.[6] Because of their relation of dependence, these four church orders are examined here, in chronological order (as nearly as this can be determined).

The final section of this paper presents the confession of the Church concerning the relation of the Office of the Holy Ministry to the celebration of the Lord's Supper in the primary liturgy of each of the five major liturgical families of antiquity. These liturgical families, their geographical region of origin, and the chief liturgy of each (the title of some being derived from the apostolic name associated with the region) have been identified by Hammond as follows:

1. The Western Syrian Family, (Jerusalem), the liturgy of St. James.
2. The Alexandrian Family, (Alexandria), the liturgy of St. Mark.

3. The Eastern Syrian Family, (Edessa), the liturgy of St. Adaeus (i.e., Addai and Mari).

4. The Hispano-Gallican Family, (Ephesus), the liturgy of St. John.

5. The Roman Family, (Rome), St. Peter, the liturgy of St. Ambrose.[7]

Instead of the liturgy of St. Ambrose, this thesis will discuss the authorized form of the Roman Mass, while referring and comparing it with the information provided in a writing of St. Ambrose. In the Hispano-Gallican family, the *Mozarabic Rite* will be analyzed. Further, a sixth liturgy will be added; namely, the liturgy of St. John Chrysostom. This liturgy is included because Byzantium-Constantinople eventually surpassed Antioch and Alexandria as both the center of Greek liturgy, and as the center of the greater part of Eastern Christendom.[8]

While this limitation of the number of liturgies considered here may be regretted, it serves to concentrate the enquiry on the most important data as well as to hold the enquiry within compassable limits. These early liturgies form the basis from which subsequent liturgies grow. As such, while by no means presenting an exhaustive discussion of this matter throughout the liturgical history of the Church, one may see here what the Church confessed of the relation of the Office of the Holy Ministry to the celebration of the Lord's Supper from as early as data is available.

With the foregoing in mind, one is clearly not able to evaluate the liturgies of the early Church without reference to the scriptural basis of that liturgical confession of faith. The prophetic and apostolic, Spirit-breathed and faith-creating words of Holy Scripture are precisely that which the Church sought to confess in her liturgies. An enquiry

12

into the relation between the Office of the Holy Ministry and the celebration of the Lord's Supper in Holy Scripture is therefore provided first.

... ye do not so much as listen to anyone, if he speak of aught else save concerning Jesus Christ in truth.[9]

Notes:

[1] Unless otherwise indicated, all English citations of the Holy Scriptures will be taken from the HOLY BIBLE, NEW INTERNATIONAL VERSION. Copyright 1973, 1978, 1984 International Bible Society. Used by permission of Zondervan Bible Publishers.

[2] Martin Luther, Small Catechism, rev. ed., (St. Louis, MO: Concordia Publishing House, 1965), vi.1-2, p. 20. The German reads: "Was ist das Sakrament des Altars?

Antwort.

Es ist der wahre Leib und Blut unsers Herrn Jesu Christi, unter dem Brot und Wein uns Christen zu essen und zu trinken von Christo selbs eingesetzt." Martin Luther, *Kleiner Katechismus*, in Die Bekenntnisschriften der evangelisch=lutherischen Kirche (Göttingen: Vanderhoeck & Ruprecht, 1986), pp. 519-520. Hereafter cited as BKS. Confessional references will be given by their place in the specific confession using standard abbreviations, and then by place in BKS. Unless otherwise noted, English citations will be taken from Theodore G. Tappert, ed., The Book of Concord (Philadelphia: Fortress Press, 1959). The standard abbreviations are as follows:

AC = The Augsburg Confession
Ap = Apology of the Augsburg Confession
SA = The Smalcald Articles
Tr = Treatise (or Tractate) on the Power and Primacy of the Pope
SC = Small Catechism
LC = Large Catechism
FC = Formula of Concord

[3] Luther, Small Catechism, p. 21. BKS, p. 520.

[4] This is not to say that the liturgies are the *only* documents wherein the early Christians' confession of faith may be seen. One finds evidence of the great seriousness with which the early Church treated the functions of the Office of the Holy Ministry, and those who served the office holders in an assisting capacity, particularly regarding the celebration of the Lord's Supper, in the canons of the church councils. One example of this is Canon XVIII of the Council of Nicæa, A.D. 325: "It has come to the knowledge of the holy and great Synod that, in some districts and cities, the deacons

administer the Eucharist to the presbyters, whereas neither canon nor custom [παρεδωκε] permits that they who have no right to offer should give the Body of Christ to them that do offer. And this also has been made known, that certain deacons now touch the Eucharist even before the bishops. Let all such practices be utterly done away, and let the deacons remain within their own bounds, knowing that they are the ministers [υπηρεται] of the bishop and the inferiors of the presbyters. Let them receive the Eucharist according to their order, after the presbyters, and let either the bishop or the presbyter administer to them. Furthermore, let not the deacons sit among the presbyters, for that is contrary to canon and order. And if, after this decree, any one shall refuse to obey, let him be deposed from the diaconate." *The Canons of the 318 Holy Fathers Assembled in the City of Nice, in Bithynia,* edited by Henry R. Percival, in Nicene and Post-Nicene Fathers, Series 2, edited by Philip Schaff and Henry Wace (Grand Rapids, MI: Wm. B. Eerdmans Publishing Company, 1988), vol. 14, p. 38. (Hereafter cited as NPNF, series no., vol. no., page no[s]). The Greek, together with Latin translation, may be found in *Concilium Nicaenum I, Canones,* Conciliorum Oecumenicorum Decreta, (Bologna, Italy: Instituto per le Scienze Religiose, 1972), pp. 14-15. This first ecumenical council treated the fact that only bishops and presbyters could celebrate ("offer") the Lord's Supper as self-evident, and they used this self-evident fact to mandate the orderly behavior of the diaconate in the context of the divine service. The sequence of ministering the body and blood of our Lord began with the Lord, and moved out from there.

[5] For a lengthy discussion of the inspiration of Scripture and related issues, see Robert Preus, The Inspiration of Scripture, 2nd ed. (London: Oliver and Boyd, 1957) and also Francis Pieper, Christian Dogmatics, vol. 1 (St. Louis, MO: Concordia Publishing House, 1950), pp. 193-367, this being the translation of Franz Pieper, Christliche Dogmatik, vol. 1 (St. Louis, MO: Concordia Publishing House, 1924), pp. 233-444. For a more concise statement of the issues involved, see the pamphlet The Inspiration of Scripture, (A Report of the Commission on Theology and Church Relations, The Lutheran Church-Missouri Synod, March 1975). For the official public doctrinal position of the Lutheran Church-Missouri Synod, the context in which the present author is working, see A Statement of Scriptural and Confessional Principles, (Adopted by The Lutheran Church-Missouri Synod, 50th Regular Convention, July 6-13, 1973; Resolution 3-01, *Proceedings,* pp. 127-128).

The foregoing presuppositions are important particularly where this paper includes references to the wealth of information included in the work of Hans Lietzmann, Mass and Lord's Supper, trans. Dorothea H. G. Reeve (Leiden: E. J. Brill, 1979), translated from Hans Lietzmann, Messe und Herrenmahl, (Bonn: A. Marcus und E. Weber's Verlag, 1926). The laudable depth of this inquiry notwithstanding, Lietzmann's thesis that "the irreconcilable duality between the conception of the Agape, or Lord's Supper, and that of the Mass, are found . . . within the New Testament itself," (p. xiii, also 330-332) is incompatible both with the above described understanding of the inspiration of Scripture, and with the information conclusively provided by early liturgical evidence. Such issues will, however, be dealt with only as necessitated by the inquiry presently being undertaken.

[6] Arthur Vööbus, The Didascalia Apostolorum in Syriac, vol. 1, tome 176 (Louvain: Corpus Scriptorum Christianorum Orientalum, 1979), p. 30.

[7] Charles E. Hammond, Liturgies Eastern and Western (London: Oxford University Press, 1878), p. xvi.

[8] Joseph A. Jungmann, The Mass of the Roman Rite: Its Origins and Development, vol. 1, trans. Francis A. Brunner (New York: Benziger Brothers, Inc., 1951), p. 42.

[9] Ignatius, Ephesians 6, in J. B. Lightfoot and J. R. Harmer, eds., The Apostolic Fathers (Grand Rapids, MI: Baker Book House, 1988), p. 139. For the Greek, see p. 107.

PART I:

THE DATA FROM HOLY SCRIPTURE

CHAPTER I

THE OFFICE OF THE HOLY MINISTRY

Old Testament Background

Prior to an examination of the relation of Old Testament "types" to the New Testament Lord's Supper, it is be helpful to note briefly the relation of the Old Testament Priesthood to the Office of the Holy Ministry in the New Testament. Next, we will examine the consequences this relationship has for understanding the administration of the forgiveness of sins.

Paul Schrieber has written a most insightful article on the subject of the Office of the Holy Ministry in the Old Testament from a confessional Lutheran perspective:

> To suggest any relationship, correlation, or application of Old Testament priesthood to the office of the ministry poses certain challenges to Lutherans, especially because of deep-seated fears of regressing to the ritualism and hierarchic clericalism of traditional Roman Catholicism. Moreover, to suggest a positive relationship is out of step with Protestantism's long-held preference for the prophetic office ("freedom of the spirit," "everyone a minister," and high ethical and social relevance of a "prophetic ministry") in opposition to the self-serving dogmatic ritualism of a ministerium whose primary goal is to maintain the status quo and preserve the "system." Such prejudice betrays a misun-

derstanding of Old and New Testament priesthood.[1]

This statement provides a valuable corrective to any such misunderstandings. It is a mistake to set the New Testament priesthood of all believers over against either the Old Testament Priesthood or the New Testament Office of the Holy Ministry. The "priesthood of all believers" (1 Peter 2:5-9) does not contradict the Office of the Holy Ministry (2 Tim. 4:1-5), any more than the "priesthood of all Israel" (Ex. 19:6) contradicted the special Aaronic Priesthood (Exodus 28-29, Leviticus 8-9).

Because of its use in reference to the New Testament Office of the Holy Ministry, the term "elder" (זקן) is most important to this study. זקן means literally a "bearded one," which may translate simply "old man," or may, as in this case, have a more technical meaning. In this latter substantive sense, the term "elders" refers to a ruling body. While Moses was on the mountain, they decided cases (Ex. 24:14). They laid their hands upon the head of the sin offering when the whole congregation sinned (Lev. 4:15). They stood with the judges before the ark at the reading of the law (Josh. 8:33). They were also given authority in civil matters.[2] The term was translated πρεσβύτερος in the Septuagint, a term which was often used of the holders of the Office of the Holy Ministry in the New Testament.

The text of Exodus 24 will be further discussed below as it concerns the relation of the sprinkling of blood upon the people in the Old Testament to the drinking of Christ's blood in the New Testament. Noteworthy at this point is the mention that this text (vv. 1-2, 9-11) makes of a certain group of seventy elders:

Then He [the LORD] said to Moses, "Come up to

the LORD, you and Aaron, Nadab and Abihu, and seventy of the elders of Israel. You are to worship at a distance, but Moses alone is to approach the LORD; the others must not come near. And the people may not come up with him."

Moses and Aaron, Nadab and Abihu, and seventy of the elders of Israel went up and saw the God of Israel. Under His feet was something like a pavement made of sapphire, clear as the sky itself. But God did not raise His hand against these leaders of the Israelites; they saw God, and they ate and drank.

Because reference is made to another group of "seventy elders" (Num. 11:16-25) in the *Apostolic Tradition*, further investigation concerning both them and these who communed with God (Ex. 24:1-2, 9-11) may prove useful.

One may begin by noting that these seventy elders were not Aaronic Priests: the establishment of this priesthood comes five chapters later (Exodus 29-30). This issue is further complicated by the fact that in Exodus 19:20-24, the Lord speaks about "priests" (כהנימ). Who were these priests, if the Aaronic Priesthood did not yet exist? Were they those to whom our text refers as "elders" (זקנימ, Num. 11:16)?

One is not able, on the basis of the scriptural evidence, to answer this last question, although an affirmative answer is certainly possible. Concerning the former question, C. F. Keil and F. Delitzsch offer the following:

> The priests were neither "the sons of Aaron," i.e. Levitical priests, nor the first-born or *principes populi*, but "those who had hitherto discharged the duties of the priestly office according to natural right and custom."[3]

One may do little better than guess as to whether or not those who were called elders would have had the "natural right and custom" of functioning as priests prior to the establishment of the Aaronic Priesthood.

Critical to this study is God's bestowing of the Spirit (which He had placed upon Moses) on seventy elders of Israel (Num. 11:16-30). One may regret that this text appears so obscure. There is no statement concerning *how* the Spirit that was on Moses was put also upon the seventy elders. The visible evidence that this had, in fact, occurred was their "prophesying" (v. 25). Keil and Delitzsch comment further:

> No account has been handed down of the further action of this committee of elders. It is impossible to determine, therefore, in what way they assisted Moses in bearing the burden of governing the people. All that can be regarded as following unquestionably from the purpose given here is, [*sic*] that they did not form a permanent body . . .[4]

However, the sources cited by these authors which contradict even this "unquestionable" conclusion suggest that it may be questionable after all.

As for the Aaronic Priesthood, Schreiber concisely presents the biblical data:

> The institution of the priesthood began when Moses consecrated Aaron who was of the tribe of Levi, and his four sons, the priesthood of the sons being subordinate to that of their father (Ex. 28). The distinct office of Aaron's priesthood is indicated by:

1) special garments (Ex. 28:2-39; Lev. 8:7-9), which were transferred to the oldest living son at the time of Aaron's death (Ex 29:29; Num. 20:25-28); 2) a special anointing (Ex. 29:7; Lev. 4:3, 5, 16; 6:19-22; 8:12; Num. 20:25-28); and 3) distinct functions, such as officiating on the Day of Atonement. Priesthood was restricted to Aaron's male and unblemished descendants, upon penalty of death (Ex. 28:43; Num. 4:15-20; 16; 18:1, 7). The Levites . . . were not to serve as priests but as auxiliary helpers. They were dedicated to this service on several grounds: 1) they had shown themselves to be zealous for Yahweh (Ex. 32:25-29); 2) they served as substitutes for the first-born sons spared in the Passover (Ex. 13:2-13; Num. 3:11-13; 8:16-18); 3) they represented Israel as a wave offering to Yahweh (Num. 8:11); and 4) they were gifts from the people to the priests (Num. 8:19).[5]

One may also note Deut. 34:9, where one reads that the office and the spirit of wisdom were bestowed upon Joshua with the laying on of Moses' hands. Eduard Lohse comments:

> Institution into office is also accomplished by the laying on of hands. One reads in P [sic] that Moses laid hands on Joshua and thus appointed him his successor. The laying on of hands is here a rite of transfer, since Joshua is thereby endued with the power he would need to discharge the office. According to Dt. 34:9 he was filled with the spirit of wisdom, . . . The transferring of this gift took place before the assembled congregation in order to ratify publicly the legitimacy of the succession, Nu. 27:21-23.

After the model of the institution of Joshua, and with express appeal to it, the Rabbis developed their own practice of ordination.[6]

To summarize: it has been seen that the Aaronic Priesthood and the "priesthood of all Israel" were both established by God, and were complementary to each other. The appointment of a certain group, with the laying on of hands upon them, to serve God as priests was an act of God's grace, not a form of discrimination against those groups not so chosen, and not a diminution of the priesthood which belonged to all Israel. Prior to the establishment of the Aaronic Priesthood there were others who served God in holy ministry, about whom less is known.

In the New Testament

The present inquiry now turns to an examination of selected texts of the New Testament pertaining to the Office of the Holy Ministry, particularly the words of Christ in John 20:21-23. The text reads as follows:

> Again Jesus said, "Peace be with you! As the Father has sent me, I am sending you." And with that He breathed on them and said, "Receive the Holy Spirit. If you forgive anyone his sins, they are forgiven; if you do not forgive them, they are not forgiven."[7]

This passage has been the source of some controversy. Donald Guthrie offers this explanation:

> The first problem is the relation this inbreathing of the Spirit has to the outpouring at Pentecost. Three different answers have been proposed.

(i) A distinction is suggested between the form 'Holy Spirit' without the article (as here and in Jn. 7:39) and the form with the article, as at Pentecost. But it is difficult to attach any meaningful significance to this distinction. It can hardly be maintained that the anarthrous form refers to the gift and the other form to the person. In any case in John 7 both forms are used side by side.

(ii) Another suggestion is that John's account is irreconcilable with Luke's, and the latter must therefore be regarded as an invention. But John's account cannot supplant the historic outpouring at Pentecost ...

(iii) This leads to the third explanation, which is the view that the breathing of the Spirit upon the disciples in John 20 must be regarded as proleptic, a foreshadowing of Pentecost. No statement is actually made that the Spirit was immediately received ...[8]

A detailed discussion of the person and work of the Holy Spirit is beyond the scope of this present work. However, Guthrie's arguments may be briefly and profitably addressed. He begins by suggesting that three answers to this perceived dilemma have been proposed. (This may be misleading, as proposed solutions number more than three, another of which will be considered shortly.) Guthrie's counter-arguments presented against the first and second theories are sound, and those theories, particularly in the form here presented, are rightly rejected. He then selects the third explanation of this text. He apparently does so by a 'process of elimination'; if the first two are incorrect, then the third must be the correct one. However, this approach is inadequate.

A more insightful analysis of this text is provided by

David Earl Holwerda. After presenting a mass of evidence, he writes:

> Therefore, we conclude that this bestowal of the Spirit is not that gift promised in the Farewell Discourses and in 7:39.
>
> This is apparent also from the nature of the gift. Jesus gave them the Spirit in connection with their commission ... Jesus is here commissioning His disciples for their official task, as He had been commissioned by the Father. As Jesus was sent into the world (17:18) to give eternal life (6:40) and thus to forgive sins (3:18), so the disciples are sent into the world (17:18) with the authority to forgive sins (20:23) and to proclaim eternal life in Christ (17:20). Because Jesus is the αποστολος of the Father, he who does not receive Him does not receive the Father (5:20). Because the disciples are the αποστολοι of Jesus, he who does not receive them does not receive Jesus (13:20). Jesus is sent with the authority of the Father, and the disciples are sent with the authority of Jesus. In this context Jesus bestows the Spirit. It is logical to conclude that the purpose of this gift is to qualify the disciples for their official task. It is to be noted that Jesus also received the Spirit to qualify Him for His office (3:34; 1:32); and it is this Spirit that the disciples received, for we read that Jesus breathed (ενεφυσησεν); i.e., Jesus did not send the Spirit from heaven (15:26) but gave the Spirit directly from Himself. This does not mean that this is another Spirit than the one received on Pentecost, for in both cases it is the Holy Spirit. In speaking of "this Spirit" we are referring to a particular activity or task of the Spirit. The task of

the Spirit in this instance is to qualify the apostles as representatives of Christ; and in virtue of this they receive the authority to forgive sins. This special gift of the Spirit was received by the apostles alone, and not by all the "brethren" as in Acts 2 . . .[9]

The reception of the Holy Spirit at one time for one purpose does not preclude the reception of the Holy Spirit at another time for another purpose. The bestowal of the Holy Spirit in John 20 was for the purpose of entrusting the apostles with the spiritual authority to forgive and retain sins. The outpouring at Pentecost was for the purpose of empowering all the believers. It is with the bestowing of the Spirit for the purpose of conferring the authority to forgive and retain sins that one is placed into the Office of the Holy Ministry. In this specific, authority-conferring sense, the Holy Spirit is uniquely given at a particular time and place, in order to put a man into the Office of the Holy Ministry. This authoritative giving of the Holy Spirit for the purpose of putting a man into the Office of the Holy Ministry appears often to have been done with the laying on of hands (1 Tim. 4:14; 5:22; 2 Tim. 1:6-7).[10] While the laying on of hands does not appear to have occurred when Jesus gave the Holy Spirit to the apostles, nothing stronger than arguments from silence can be advanced to suggest that it was ever omitted when a man was put into the office subsequent to the initial office bestowing event in John 20.

Notes:

[1] Paul L. Schrieber, "Priests Among Priests: The Office of the Ministry in Light of the Old Testament Priesthood," Concordia Journal 14 (July 1988):215.

[2] R. Laird Harris, Theological Wordbook of the Old Testament, 2 vols. (Chicago: The Moody Press, 1980), vol. 1, pp. 249-250. (Hereafter "TWOT").

[3] C. F. Keil and F. Delitzsch, Commentary on the Old Testament, 10 vols. (Grand Rapids, MI: William B. Eerdmans Publishing Co., 1985), vol. 1, trans. James Martin, part ii, p. 103.

[4] Keil and Delitzsch, 1:iv.72

[5] Schrieber, p. 217.

[6] Gerhard Kittel, ed., Theological Dictionary of the New Testament, vol. 9, trans. Geoffrey W. Bromiley (Grand Rapids, MI: Wm. B. Eerdmans Publishing Company, 1987), s.v. Eduard Lohse, χειρ, p. 429. Commenting on Acts 6:6, Lohse asserts that "it may be assumed with a high degree of probability that Jewish Christianity in Palestine . . ." had adopted the above mentioned Rabbinic practice "and was using the laying on of hands for institution to office." p. 433.

[7] The Missouri Synod's 1943 version of Luther's Small Catechism quotes this text, and then asks, "What do you believe according to these words?" The following answer is provided: "I believe that, when the called ministers of Christ deal with us by His divine command, especially when they exclude manifest and impenitent sinners from the Christian congregation, and, again, when they absolve those who repent of their sins and are willing to amend, this is as valid and certain, in heaven also, as if Christ, our dear Lord, dealt with us Himself." Martin Luther, Small Catechism, rev. ed. (St. Louis, MO: Concordia Publishing House, 1965), p. 18, italics added. This citation does not appear in the critical editions of the Book of Concord, and an investigation into the origins of this text is beyond the scope of this paper. This citation is, however, a part of the Small Catechism as generally in use in the Missouri Synod. It refers the Lord's bestowing of the Holy Spirit and the authority to forgive and to retain sins not only to the ten apostles to whom these words were originally spoken, but also to all "called ministers of Christ." See also AC XXVIII.5-7 for a text in the Book of Concord which confesses John 20:21-23 in much the same way. Here, the "power the keys" (Gewalt der Schlussel) is used interchangeably with "the power of bishops." Tappert, p. 81; BKS, p. 121. This verse is also cited at several points in the Tractate to demonstrate that the apostles were entrusted strictly with spiritual authority, and not a this-worldly political authority.

[8] Donald Guthrie, New Testament Theology (Downers Grove, IL: InterVarsity Press, 1981), pp. 533-534.

[9] David Earl Holwerda, The Holy Spirit and Eschatology in the Gospel of John (Kampen: J. H. Kok N. V., 1959), pp. 23-25.

[10]After an examination of these three verses, Scaer summarizes with fourteen points, and then offers a concluding sentence:

"1.   Ordination as a ceremony through which persons are admitted into the office of pastor, (indicated as <u>presbuteros</u>) is mentioned three times in the Pastoral Epistles.

2.   In all three citations the laying on of hands is mentioned as part of the rite.

3.   Those actively participating in the rite are only those who already possess the office into which the recipient is being ushered.

4.   Through the activity of this rite, a <u>charisma</u>, a gift or endowment, is given to the recipient.

5.   The gift is given at one time and in one act. No repetition of the act is mentioned.

6.   The gift exists continually within the recipient.

7.   The gift may fall into disuse and be revitalized by its possessor.

8.   Though the gift is given through the laying on of the hands, God is the Giver of the gift.

9.   The gift is not available to any Christian for the asking but is to be given to those who have met certain criteria.

10.   Ordination is a rite whose misapplication carries a threat.

11.   It is a rite through which those who bestow it share in the ministry of the one who receives it.

12.   The gift given in the rite is identified as the Holy Spirit bestowing certain gifts.

13.   It is a rite which is encompassed within an apostolic command.

14.   It is a rite which Paul enjoins upon Timothy to continue. Paul is not giving instructions for [a] one time limited situation.

"I personally find it very difficult to designate as a human rite or adiaphoron any ceremony in which God is the Giver and the Holy Spirit is the recipient [gift?], which can only be administered under certain stringent conditions, which carries with it a threat, which makes the acting participant in the rite responsible for the activities of the recipient of the rite, and which gives the recipient a gift which remains."

David Scaer, <u>Ordination: Human Rite or Divine Ordinance</u> (Fort Wayne, IN: Concordia Theological Seminary Press, n.d.), pp. 11-12. For a lengthier discussion of the laying on of hands in the New Testament, see Edward J. Kilmartin, "Ministry and Ordination in Early Christianity against a Jewish Background," <u>Studia Liturgica</u> 13 (1979): 42-69. An even broader

28

examination of this subject may be found in Eduard Lohse, <u>Die Ordination im Spätjudentum und im Neuen Testament</u> (Gottingen: Vanderhoeck & Ruprecht, 1951). Lohse distinguishes between the laying on of hands for the purpose of ordaining (as in the pastoral epistles), and those instances in which the laying on of hands appears to have amounted to imparting a blessing (as is usually the case when it is mentioned in Acts), pp. 69-84. He concludes that it is inappropriate to label ordination an "adiaphoron," p. 101.

CHAPTER II

THE LORD'S SUPPER

Old Testament Background

Perhaps the first point to be made regarding the Old Testament background of the Lord's Supper is a word of caution. When the Lord instituted His Supper, His words, "this is My blood of the [new] covenant," (Matt. 26:28) refer back to Exodus 24:8: "Moses then took the blood, sprinkled it on the people and said, "This is the blood of the covenant that the Lord has made with you in accordance with all these words." Joachim Jeremias has argued persuasively that the Last Supper was, in fact, a Passover meal.[1] Sverre Aalen understands 1 Cor. 10:3-4 as connecting the drinking of water from the rock and the eating of manna with the Lord's Supper, going so far as to call the former "das alttestamentliche Abendmahl."[2] In any case, it is apparent that the Lord, in instituting the Lord's Supper, and St. Paul, in handing it on, did not simply modify a single Old Testament practice for New Testament use, but gave the Church something new, albeit endowed with references to, and in continuity with, several Old Testament events and practices. While these Old Testament events and practices may inform the celebration of the Lord's Supper, one may not establish the doctrine of the Lord's Supper or its celebration exclusively by way of an analogical appeal to an Old Testament practice.

Of the three possible "types" of the Lord's Supper that have just been mentioned, a direct connection is found between the Lord's words of institution and the Exodus 24 passage. Hummel makes the following observation:

> The first phase of the Sinaitic revelation climaxes in the impressive covenant ratification ceremony of chap. 24. We have here (in the very presence of God!) both a sacred meal and a sacrifice with a unique blood ceremony, both elements fulfilled as Christ establishes His Supper, the Eucharist, as the "new covenant in My blood" (Matt. 26:28; cf. Heb. 9:18-21).[3]

There is no indication in Scripture that the sprinkling of blood upon the people was ever repeated.[4] Already, then, one encounters a point at which formulating the doctrine of the Lord's Supper by way of analogy with the sprinkling of blood in the Old Testament simply will not work.

William Dallmann provides an orderly presentation of the parallels between the Passover in the Old Testament and the Lord's Supper in the New Testament:

> 1. In the Old Testament the Passover was to be a lamb, Ex. 12:3.
>
> In the New Testament our Passover is Christ "the Lamb of God," John 1:29, 36, and in about forty more passages.
>
> 2. The Old Testament Paschal lamb was to be "without blemish," Ex. 12:5.
>
> The New Testament Paschal lamb is a "lamb without blemish and without spot," I Peter 1:19, "holy, harmless, undefiled, separate from sinners."
>
> 3. Of the Old Testament lamb we read: "The whole assembly shall kill it," Ex. 12:6.
>
> "Who killed the Lord Jesus," we read concerning the Jews in I Thess. 2:15. "Worthy is the Lamb that was

slain," Rev. 5:6-12.[5]

4. In the Old Testament the Paschal lamb was a sacrifice and an offering: "It is the sacrifice of the Lord's Passover," Ex. 12:27.

So in the New Testament, "Christ, our Passover, is sacrificed for us," I Cor. 5:7.

"We are sanctified through the offering of the body of Jesus Christ once for all." Heb. 10:8-10; 9:14.

5. The Old Testament commanded the eating:— "Thus shall ye eat it," Ex. 12:11.

The New Testament commands eating:—"Take, eat," said our Lord.

6. In the Old Testament a natural lamb was eaten in the natural way, "And they shall eat the flesh in that night," Ex. 12:8.

In the New Testament a supernatural Lamb is eaten in a supernatural way, for the unworthy eater is guilty of the Lord's body, I Cor. 11:27, 29.

7. In the Paschal Supper the Jews received bread and the body of the lamb; in the New Testament the communicants received bread and the body of the Lamb of God.

8. In the Old Testament the body of a typical lamb was received; in the New Testament the body of the true Lamb is received.

10 [*sic.*]. In the Old Testament Supper there was real bread and real eating in a natural manner; in the New Testament there is real bread and real eating in a natural manner.

11. In the Old Testament there was real flesh and real eating in a natural manner; in the New Testament there is real flesh and real eating of that real flesh but

in a supernatural manner.

12. In the Old Testament we find the real shedding of the real blood of the typical lamb; in the New Testament we find the real shedding of the real blood of the true Lamb of God.

13. The blood of the Old Testament lamb was shed for bodily salvation: "When I see the blood I will pass over you, and the plague shall not rest on you."

The blood of the New Testament Lamb is shed for spiritual salvation: "This is my blood, shed for you for the remission of sins."

14. In the Old Testament the unworthy communicant brought on himself bodily destruction: "whosoever eateth leavened bread, that soul shall be cut off from Israel."

In the New Testament the unworthy communicant brings on himself spiritual destruction:"He that eateth and drinketh unworthily, eateth and drinketh damnation to himself, not discerning the Lord's body," I Cor. 11:29.

15. In the Old Testament the Passover was a feast: "Ye shall keep it a feast;" in the New Testament it is also a feast: "Christ our Passover is sacrificed for us, therefore let us keep the feast," I Cor. 5:8.

16. The Passover was a memorial of the freedom from the bodily slavery in Egypt:"This day shall be unto you for a memorial"; the Lord's Supper is a memorial of the freedom from the spiritual slavery in sin gained for us by our Savior: "This do in remembrance of me," Luke 22:19.

17. In the Old Testament the Passover was only for members of the Church: "There shall no stranger eat

thereof," Ex. 12:43. In the New Testament the Lord's Supper is only for the true disciples of Christ: "Let a man examine himself, and so let him eat," I Cor. 11:28.

18. [Omitted by the present author]

19. As in the Old Testament the command went forth: "All the congregation of Israel shall keep it" (Heb. do it), Ex. 12:47, so in the New Testament the command went forth: "Drink ye all of it," Matt. 26:27.

20. In the Old Testament we read: "It is a night to be much observed unto the Lord for bringing them out from the land of Egypt," Ex. 12:42; in the New Testament we read: "This do in remembrance of me," I Cor. 11:25. "Show the Lord's death till He come," I Cor. 11:26.[6]

To be sure, one may consider some of the above argumentation to be a little forced. Nevertheless, the conclusion that the Lord's Supper in the New Testament fulfills the Old Testament Passover is difficult to avoid.

In the New Testament

It has been seen that the words spoken by the Lord on the night in which He was betrayed refer back to the sprinkling of blood on the people in Exodus 24. This Old Testament precursor to the Lord's Supper does serve to remind one that the Lord's Supper is not, in the final analysis, "repeated," either. It is better to say that it is continued; that which the Lord said and did on the night in which He was betrayed continues wherever His mandate "this do" is observed. As it was on that night, so it continues to be that the true celebrant at any celebration of the Lord's Supper is the Lord Jesus Christ Himself. Understood as such, this volume is really investigating the question of whom the Lord has entrusted to be the instrument by which He continues to celebrate His Supper. The use of the term "celebrant" in this book is therefore to be understood as referring to the instrument of the Lord, not as indicating some sort of a replacement for the absent Lord (for He is not absent!), nor as another mediator between God and His Testament people (1 Tim. 2:5, Heb. 12:24).

To repeat, it has been seen that the words which the Lord spoke on the night in which He was betrayed were spoken in the context of a Passover meal. The implications of this for the celebration of the Lord's Supper will be further discussed below (see Chapter IV).

Concerning the doctrine of the Lord's Supper itself, the reader is again reminded that it is not our intended purpose to present and defend the Lutheran doctrine of the Lord's Supper. It is presupposed that the Lutheran doctrine is, in fact, the Scriptural one. For an explanation of that doctrine, one can do little better than to examine the words which Christ spoke over the bread and wine (Matt. 26:26-29; Mark 14:22-25; Luke 22:15-20; 1 Cor. 11:23-25), and hear again from the *Small Catechism*:

> What is the benefit of such eating and drinking?
>
> That is shown us by these words, "Given and shed for you for the remission of sins"; namely, that in the Sacrament forgiveness of sins, life and salvation are given us through these words. For where there is forgiveness of sins, there is also life and salvation.[7]

The words of Christ include the promise "for the forgiveness of sins." This will be critical in the discussion of the relationship between the Office of the Holy Ministry to the celebration of the Lord's Supper which follows in Chapter IV.

Notes:
[1] Joachim Jeremias, The Eucharistic Words of Jesus, trans. Norman Perrin (Philadelphia: Fortress Press, 1986), pp. 41-88. See Matt. 26:17-19, Mark 14:12-16, Luke 22:7-16.
[2] Sverre Aalen, "Das Abendmahl als Opfermahl bei Paulus," Novum Testamentum 6 (1963):132
[3] Horace D. Hummel, The Word Becoming Flesh (St. Louis, MO: Concordia Publishing House, 1979), p. 76.
[4] The blood was put upon those ordained to the Aaronic Priesthood (Ex. 29:19-21, Leviticus 8-9).
[5] See also in this regard Acts 2:22-23, 7:51-53.
[6] William Dallmann, The Real Presence (Pittsburgh, PA: American Lutheran Publication Board, 1900), pp. 14-18.
[7] Luther, Small Catechism, p. 21. BKS, p. 520.

CHAPTER III

THE RELATION OF THE OFFICE OF THE HOLY MINISTRY TO THE FORGIVENESS OF SINS

Old Testament Background

The Lord's entrusting the administration of His means of forgiving sins to a select group of people is not unique to the New Testament. In fact, the evidence of men being placed in such a role may be even more readily recognized in the Old Testament. Christianity is not the 'replacement religion' instituted after the termination of the religion revealed in the Old Testament; rather, Christianity is the rightful continuation of that religion (Acts 3:13-26; Rom. 1:2; 3:21-26; 15:4; 1 Cor. 15:3-4; Col. 2:9-12; Heb. 1:1-2). For this reason, the inclusion of a brief examination of the connection of the Old Testament priesthood to the administration of forgiveness, particularly the placing of the blood of the Testament upon the people of Israel, is not entirely anachronistic.

David Chytraeus (a Lutheran theologian of the sixteenth century) puts the relation of the Old Testament to the New in a scriptural and typically Lutheran way, calling the Old Testament Levitical sacrifices "sacraments," in that they were connected with the forgiveness of sins. He also indicates that they were marks of the Old Testament "Church."[1] It is clear from the text of Leviticus (1-8) that, while the whole people of Israel was involved in these sacrificial rites, the 'celebrants' were the priests. The priesthood of all Israel and the Office of the Aaronic Priesthood were not contradictory, but rather complementary to each other.

Paul Schrieber summarizes the relation of the Old Testament Priesthood to the forgiveness of sins, and connects this with the New Testament:

> Of course, apart from the vicarious atonement and priesthood of Christ, of which these Old Testament institutions were types, none of them would have been of any value. On this side of the cross the sacramental ministry continues, with its focus on the sacrifice of Christ. It is now the privilege of those in the office of the ministry to administer the means of grace, the washing of holy Baptism and the body and blood of Christ for the forgiveness of sins. All the Old Testament priests ever touched was the flesh and blood of bulls and goats.
>
> Nonetheless, Old Testament priests did convey God's forgiveness to those who confessed their sins and offered the proper sacrifices. Upon judging the acceptability of a sacrifice the priest presided over the rituals by which atonement was made and sins were absolved (Lev. 1:4; 5:16; 19:7; 22:17-25). The Aaronic Benediction (Num. 6:22-27) likewise served as an actual conferral of God's blessing, grace, peace, and forgiveness on Israel. In so blessing the people, the priests had the privilege of "placing the name of Yahweh" upon the people.[2]

The ministry of forgiveness with which the priests had been entrusted was not, however, controlled by the priest. It was *Yahweh's* priesthood. His words mandated what was to be done, and what was not. The Lord jealously guarded

His holy priesthood, visiting fatal consequences upon the heads of Aaron's sons when they undertook to offer to the Lord "unauthorized fire" (Lev. 10:1-3).

While the priesthood belonged properly to the Lord, it was not to be exercised by those to whom the Lord had not given it. The connection between the office of priest and officiating at sacrifices, atoning or otherwise, was absolute. Saul was cut off as Israel's king for presuming to offer sacrifices to the Lord, which thing had not been entrusted to him to do (1 Samuel 15).

Faith does not seek to improve upon what the Lord gives. What the Lord gave to the Aaronic Priesthood to do, the faithful priests did faithfully, and the faithful people faithfully received their doing of it. This was not only true for the Old Testament priesthood, but for the New Testament Office of the Holy Ministry as well.

In the New Testament

To attempt to discuss the Office of the Holy Ministry in one chapter and then to discuss the relation of that office to the forgiveness of sins in another chapter is difficult at best. It has already been seen in Chapter I that the office was specifically instituted for the purpose of forgiving and retaining sins. Nevertheless, some additional information is presented here in order to shed further light on this subject. Several verses of the New Testament merit special consideration in this connection.

To begin, one may note that in discussing the New Testament Office of the Holy Ministry, there is only one ministry being discussed, and this ministry includes both the apostles and the elders/bishops (c.f. 1 Cor. 3:5-9; Heb. 13:17, 24; Tit. 1:5-7; 1 Peter 5:1-2. In the latter two references the terms "elder" [πρεσβυτερος, sometimes translated "presbyter"] and "overseer" [εφπισκοπος, sometimes translated "bishop"] are used interchangeably).

Next, one reads in 1 Cor. 4:1: "So then, men ought to regard us as servants of Christ and as those entrusted [οικονομοις] with the secret things [μυστηριων] of God." The first question to be asked is, "Who is the 'us' to whom St. Paul refers?" Clearly, it includes Paul himself. The names immediately preceding (1 Cor. 3:22) are Paul, Apollos, and Cephas (i.e., Peter). That Peter and Paul held the Office of the Holy Ministry is well known. Apollos was also a preacher in the early Church (Acts 18:24-19:1; 1 Cor. 1:12). In any case, Paul does not refer here to the Church at large, but rather to those holding the Office of the Holy Ministry.

Otto Michel observes that in 1 Cor. 4:1, Paul uses the word οικονομοις "as a figure for apostolic authority and knowledge ... [Paul] links 'ministers of Christ' and 'stewards of the mysteries.'"[3] The technical usage of μυστηριον ("mystery") as a term for the sacraments is a post-New Testament development.[4] As such, the phrase "stewards of the mysteries" may not be exclusively equated with "stewards of the sacraments." Its content is all that God had in mind to do to fulfill His promise of salvation; everything which Jesus did and manifested and entrusted to His apostles to be preached in His name to all nations beginning at Jerusalem (Luke 24:44-48). "The plural is used to denote Christian preaching by the apostles and teachers" in 1 Cor. 4:1.[5] C. F. W. Walther confesses the preaching of the Gospel as combined with the administration of the sacraments. This is understandable, as preaching is the verbal administration of the Gospel, and administering the sacraments is the physical administration of the Gospel. Werner Elert observes, "the

administration of the sacraments and the church's procla-
mation are inseparable, since these are constitutive of the
church only when they are kept together."[6] Walther cites 1
Cor. 4:1 in this context,[7] and a reference by Peter Bläser to
this verse is noted below in Chapter IV.

The final passage to be considered here is 2 Cor.
3:1-6. Particularly important are verses 5-6a: "Not that we
are competent in ourselves to claim anything for ourselves,
but our competence comes from God. He has made us
competent as ministers [διακονους] of a new covenant
[διαθηκης] ..."

R. C. H. Lenski connects these verses with 1 Cor.
4:1, and then proceeds to offer a correction of this translation:

> All believers are named as the heirs who are to be
> paid out with all the gospel blessings. We may call the
> ministers of God the administrators (I Cor. 4:1), yet
> they themselves are heirs. So in the New Testament
> διαθηκη="testament." And we should render, not
> "ministers of a new testament," but as one concept:
> "new testament ministers."[8]

The term διαθηκη (translated by the New
International Version as "covenant" but probably more
aptly rendered "testament"[9]) is the same term found in
the words of institution where the Lord mandates the
drinking of "the new διαθηκη in My blood." Paul speaks
in the first person plural of God having made "us competent
as new testament ministers." Two questions may be asked:
Who are those to whom Paul refers as 'us' as distinct from
'you,' and what does it mean that they are new testament
"ministers"?

The term διακονεω carries the original sense of
"to wait at table."[10] Paul, however, includes himself as one
of these "ministers," and it is clear from Acts 6:2 that those
who have been called to the Ministry of the Word (τον
λογον του θεου διακονειν) are to attend to their calling,
which is exclusive of waiting on tables (τραπεζαις). Thus,
the reference here is taken to refer to several men who hold
the Office of the Holy Ministry, perhaps including Timothy
and Erastus (see Acts 19:22) along with Paul himself.

Much of what is written in 2 Corinthians 2-6 deals
with the Office of the Holy Ministry. Further evidence of
the divine establishment of the Office of the Holy Ministry
may be found in these chapters. For example, the final verse
of 2 Cor. 2(:17b) reads, "as commissioned by God, in the sight
of God we speak in Christ."[11] The following may be found
in 1 Cor. 5:18-21:

> All this is from God, who through Christ reconciled
> us to Himself and gave us the ministry of reconcilia-
> tion; that is, God was in Christ reconciling the world
> to Himself, not counting their trespasses against them,
> and entrusting to us the message of reconciliation. So
> we are ambassadors for Christ, God making His appeal
> through us. We beseech you on behalf of Christ, be
> reconciled to God. For our sake He made Him to be
> sin who knew no sin, so that in Him we might become
> the righteousness of God. (RSV)

Thus one sees in the New Testament that the Office of the
Holy Ministry is the office of reconciliation, of forgiving
and retaining sins.

From Eph. 4:32 we see that this does not mean that
there may never come a time in which one who is not "called

and ordained" may forgive the sins of another. On the basis of Matt. 18:20 ("For where two or three are gathered together in my name, there am I with them,") the *Treatise on the Power and Primacy of the Pope*, 67 confesses, "So, in an emergency even a layman absolves and becomes the minister and pastor of another."[12] The emergency assumption of the office, however, is not to be equated either with acting apart from it, or with presuming thereby to lay permanent claim to it. In an emergency, a layman may become an *ad hoc* holder of the Office of the Holy Ministry. In any case, the forgiving and retaining of sins does not become detached from that office.

Notes:

[1] David Chytraeus, On Sacrifice, trans. John Warwick Montgomery (St. Louis, MO: Concordia Publishing House, 1962), pp. 60-62.

[2] Paul L. Schrieber, "Priests Among Priests: The Office of the Ministry in Light of the Old Testament Priesthood," Concordia Journal 14 (July 1988):218-219.

[3] Gerhard Kittel, ed., Theological Dictionary of the New Testament, vol. 5, trans. Geoffrey W. Bromiley (Grand Rapids, MI: Wm. B. Eerdmans Publishing Company, 1987), s.v. Otto Michel, οικονομος, p. 150-151. (Hereafter "TDNT").

[4] Bornkamm, μυστηριον, TDNT 4:826-827.

[5] Walter Bauer, A Greek-English Lexicon of the New Testament and Other Early Christian Literature, trans. William F. Arndt and F. Wilbur Gingrich, revised F. Wilbur Gingrich and Frederick W. Danker (Chicago: University of Chicago Press, 1979), p. 530. (Hereafter "BAGD").

[6] Werner Elert, The Lord's Supper Today, trans. Martin Bertram and Rudolph F. Norden (St. Louis, MO: Concordia Publishing House, 1973), pp. 45-46.

[7] C. F. W. Walther, Church and Ministry, trans. J. T. Mueller (St. Louis, MO: Concordia Publishing House, 1987), p. 213.

[8] R. C. H. Lenski, The Interpretation of St. Paul's First and Second Epistles to the Corinthians (Minneapolis, MN: Augsburg Publishing House, 1963), p. 920.

[9] Thus Barnes suggests that "the writers of the New Testament never meant to represent the transaction between God and man as a compact or

44

covenant properly so called. They have studiously avoided it . . ." Albert
Barnes, Notes on the Epistle to the Hebrews, revised ed. (London: George
Routledge and Sons, n.d.), p. 184. Had the writers of the New Testament
intended to express such a joint partnership, a most appropriate term was
readily available, namely συνθηκη.

[10] Herman W. Beyer, διακονεω, in TDNT 2:84.

[11] Cited from The Holy Bible, Revised Standard Version (Grand Rapids,
MI: Zondervan Publishing House, 1952).

[12] Tr.67; Tappert, p. 331; BKS, p. 491.

CHAPTER IV

THE SCRIPTURAL EVIDENCE OF THE
RELATION OF THE OFFICE OF THE HOLY
MINISTRY TO THE CELEBRATION OF THE
LORD'S SUPPER

The Holy Scriptures introduce neither the New Testament Office of the Holy Ministry nor the Lord's Supper in isolation; rather, they are introduced against the backdrop of the Old Testament. Little can be said on the basis of the Old Testament that serves independently to establish any part of the New Testament doctrine of the relation of the Office of the Holy Ministry to the celebration of the Lord's Supper. The Old Testament priesthood of all Israel did not contradict or prevent the divine assignment of certain functions, particularly the ritual distribution of the forgiveness of sins, to the Office of Elder or to the Priesthood of Aaron; the New Testament priesthood of all believers may not be presumed to proscribe the divine assignment of special functions to those God calls to the office entrusted with performing them, either. The Old Testament provides less information concerning the role of the elder, but the New Testament refers to those who hold the Office of the Holy Ministry as elders (presbyters), not as priests. Old Testament rites cited in passages of the New Testament which deal with the Lord's Supper may *inform* the doctrine of the relation of the Office of the Holy Ministry to the celebration of the Lord's Supper, but they cannot *establish* that doctrine.

Christ instituted the Office of the Holy Ministry.[1] He entrusted the holders of that office with the preaching and teaching of the Gospel, specifically the forgiving and retaining of sins (John 20:21-23—see Chapter I; see also Luke 24:47). This includes the celebration of the Lord's Supper, because the Lord's Supper is a means through which God forgives sins. The institution accounts, therefore, become crucial to a consideration of the relation of this office to the celebration of the Lord's Supper.

In the account of the institution of the Lord's Supper found in Matthew 26, one notes that the Lord's Supper is "for the forgiveness of sins." This is from the Lord; He has said so. Scripture speaks only of the apostles being present when the Lord's Supper was first instituted (26:20). It was entrusted to them. Much has been written concerning the nature of this entrusting of the Lord's Supper to the apostles. Hermann Sasse writes:

> The passage where the Roman Church believes it has found its priesthood, the office of the priest who offers the sacrifice of the Mass, is the words of our Lord at the Last Supper: "This do in remembrance of Me." Where is there anything about sacrifice there? Where is there even a hint that this was an ordination? How can one understand Jesus' command to repeat in such a way that from now on the apostles and the priests to be ordained by them should sacrifice the body and blood of our Lord for the living and the dead? Something is being read into the New Testament that is not there.[2]

The context of this statement must be carefully considered. Sasse is refuting the Roman doctrine of the sacrifice of the Mass, particularly the idea that there is, in the words of institution, a scriptural basis for this teaching. He makes the point that this is not the beginning of a chain of ordinations, least of all the initiation of a priesthood charged with sacrificing "the body and blood of our Lord for the living and the dead." Thus Sasse rejects the assertion that this is an ordination in that specific sense. Nevertheless, it is clear that the Lord is entrusting His Supper to the apostles, albeit for the sake of the Church. It would be wrong to ask, "Is the Lord's Supper here entrusted to the apostles, or to the Church?" The answer is "Yes"; it is a "both/and," not an "either/or."

The close connection of the Office of the Holy Ministry and the Lord's Supper may be seen from St. Paul's words in 1 Cor. 11:23: "For I received from the Lord what I also passed on to you: The Lord Jesus, on the night He was betrayed, took bread . . ." The wording of the Greek is important here: "Εγω γαρ παρελαβον απο του κυριου, ο και παρεδωκα υμιν, οτι ο κυριος Ιησους εν τη νυκτι η παρεδιδετο ελαβεν αρτον . . ." Not only is the personal pronoun εγω grammatically unnecessary, but it is also curious that St. Paul would mention himself ("I") before he mentions anything else, including the Lord Jesus. The word order is important in Greek. The use of the pronoun "I," particularly in this position, is therefore understood as emphatic. The Lord's Supper does not exist as an abstraction. The doing of it, and the handing on of it, only occur as it is done and handed on by one who has been entrusted with doing it and with entrusting it to others to do.

There is good reason to believe that the account of the Lord's Supper which follows (1 Cor. 11:23b-26) was quoted by St. Paul from the liturgy.[3] The question centers around the understanding of "Εγω γαρ παρελαβον απο του κυριου." Is this to be understood as a direct revelation from God to St. Paul, or is this to be understood as indicating that St. Paul received these words of the Lord as the liturgy had derived them from what the Lord did and said on the night in which He was betrayed? Hans Lietzmann proposes a mediating position, that Paul was familiar with the tradition, but "the essential meaning of this story" was revealed by the Lord directly to the apostle.[4] If, as Sasse implies,[5] St. Paul is citing the words from the liturgy of the Lord's Supper, then an early connection of his Apostolic Office and the Lord's Supper may be seen here. The Lord entrusted him with the celebration of His Supper, and the apostle thus gave the celebration of it on to the Church in Corinth. The celebrant would have been one of those who had been entrusted with the office of stewardship over those things which God had revealed.

One further point concerning this verse: St. Paul's technical use of the word παρεδωκα ("I passed down" or "handed on") is of great importance. It is the verbal form of the noun παραδοσις, or "tradition"; that is, "that which is handed down." Friedrich Büchsel comments further:

> For Paul, Christian teaching is tradition (1 C.11:2; 2 Th.2:15; 3:6; cf. 1 C.11:23; 15:1-11), and he demands that the churches should keep to it, since salvation depends on it (1 C.15:2). He sees no antithesis between pneumatic piety and the high estimation of tradition. The essential point for Paul is that it has been handed down (1 C.15:3), and that it derives from the Lord (11:23). A tradition initiated by himself or others is without validity (Col.2:8).[6]

For the apostle, all teaching can be traced to one of

two sources: either it is a tradition (παραδοσις) originating with man (κατα ανθρωπον, Col. 2:8), or it is απο του κυριου, from the Lord. Only that which belongs to the latter category of παραδοσις is reliable. This is what the Apostle hands on, and this alone is to be received by the Church. In context, one sees that this is most particularly the case when it comes to the Lord's Supper.

This may be seen still more clearly with the help of Peter Bläser, who makes three general points concerning the relation of the Office of the Holy Ministry and the Lord's Supper in the New Testament.[7] These may be roughly summarized as follows: 1) The apostle (and the holder of the "ecclesiastical office" [das kirchliche Amt]) has a special mandate as the representative of Christ and steward of the mysteries (1 Cor. 4:1). 2) Particularly in St. Paul's writings, both Baptism and the Lord's Supper have a fundamental meaning in making the person receiving them a member of the Body of Christ (1 Cor. 11:25-27, 12:13). 3) By way of the Apostolic Office, there are certain formal evidences in the New Testament of a connection between office (Amt) and the Lord's Supper (Eucharistie).

Several pieces of evidence are adduced in regard to this last point. The first is the use of the Greek verb ποιειν in the institution narratives. Bläser cites the Septuagint translation of several pertinent texts of the Hebrew Scriptures. The following are specifically mentioned:[8]

> Do [Grk: ποιησεις] for Aaron and his sons everything I have commanded you, taking seven days to ordain them. (Exodus 29:35)

> Each bull or ram, each lamb or young goat, is to be prepared in this manner. Do [Grk: ποιησεις] this

for each one, for as many as you prepare.

Everyone who is native-born must do [Grk:ποιησει] these things in this way when he brings an offering made by fire as an aroma pleasing to the Lord. (Numbers 15:11-13)

His brother's widow shall go up to him in the presence of the elders, take off one of his sandals, spit in his face and say, "This is what is done [Grk: ποιησουσιν] to the man who will not build up his brother's family line." (Deuteronomy 25:9)

Concerning the Hebrew word 'asâ, the following definition is offered:

Aside from the numerous occurrences of the meaning "do" or "make" in a general sense, 'asâ is often used with the sense of ethical obligation. The covenant people were frequently commanded to "do" all that God had commanded (Ex 23:22; Lev 19:37; Deut 6:18, etc.). The numerous contexts in which this concept occurs attest to the importance of an ethical response to God which goes beyond mere mental abstraction and which is translatable into obedience which is evidenced in demonstrable act.[9]

This is the theological "freight" that it is suggested the Greek word ποιειτε carries in the dominical mandate "do this in remembrance of Me" (1 Cor. 11:24-25). The verb employed where Christ says, "I am going to celebrate the Passover . . ." (NIV), is, once again, ποιω (Matt. 26:18). His command, "Do this," was addressed to those present at the time, namely, the apostles. This is cited as the only occurrence of this verb in connection with a commanded cultic action in the New Testament.[10]

Additional evidence for the connection of the Office of the Holy Ministry and the celebration of the Lord's Supper is derived from the indications that the Last Supper was a Passover meal.[11] It was the responsibility of the *paterfamilias* to speak the words of explanation; this was not simply a duty assigned at random to one of those present.[12] Jesus Himself was the *paterfamilias* at the Last Supper.[13] The command to "do this" is specifically connected with the eating of the bread and the drinking of the wine, but this could not be done without the words of institution being put upon the elements. One knows what the elements are only as a word of the Lord is put upon them. The one entrusted with being the Lord's instrument for placing His words upon the elements takes on the role of *paterfamilias* at the celebration of the Lord's Supper. He acts in the stead and by the mandate of the Lord Jesus Christ, the true *paterfamilias*, whose words are to be spoken.[14]

Included in the words of institution is the Gospel promise, "for the forgiveness of sins." Because of this, it would be inappropriate at best for one to whom the office of the forgiving and the retaining of sins had not been given to speak these words. References to "the breaking of bread" in Acts and in the Epistles are generally understood to be references to the celebration of the Lord's Supper.[15] In Acts 20:7-12 the celebrant was the Apostle Paul. No example of a "lay-celebrant" is to be found in the New Testament.

This 'new testament' about which Paul speaks in 2 Cor. 3:6 is not detached from the blood of that new testament about which Christ speaks in His words in the night of His betrayal. It follows that those who serve as the Lord's instruments for administering the blood of the new testament are those whom the Lord has called to the New Testament ministry, that is, those whom "He has made competent" as ministers of the New Testament.

To summarize the scriptural evidence concerning the relation of the celebration of the Lord's Supper to the Office of the Holy Ministry: In the New Testament one finds that the holder of the Office of the Holy Ministry is entrusted with the spiritual authority to forgive and retain sins "in the stead and by the mandate" of the Lord Jesus Christ Himself. Included with this authority is the celebration of the Lord's Supper, because this is a means by which sins are forgiven and, when communion is refused to a would-be communicant for reason of manifest and unrepented sins, retained. A lay-celebration of the Lord's Supper lacks both a divine mandate and any scriptural precedent. The connection of the Last Supper with the Passover meal further suggests that the role of *paterfamilias* is not to be capriciously exercised by just anyone, but by one who has been called by the Lord through the congregation to serve them in the Office of the Holy Ministry. Because the celebration of the Lord's Supper is a specific exercise of the forgiving and the retaining of sins, only one to whom this office has been entrusted is to exercise it in this way. With no scripturally envisioned scenario of an "emergency Lord's Supper," a proper understanding of the exercise of this "churchly office" is not further complicated by such a contingency. The Church acts to administer the Lord's Supper when it puts a man into the office which has the dominical mandate to celebrate it. Scripture does not address questions concerning what is, or is not, given or received when one presumes to celebrate the Lord's Supper without having been entrusted with the spiritual authority to do so by the Lord through the call of His Church.

Notes:

[1] Present limitations require that the present author proceed on the basis of this presupposition, rather than defending it at length. For one recent defense of the view that ordination is a divine ordinance, see the citation of David Scaer's article in note 10, Chapter I. Where ordination is understood to be a divine ordinance, the conclusion that the Office of the Holy Ministry is of dominical/apostolic origin is unavoidable.

[2] Hermann Sasse, We Confess the Sacraments, trans. Norman Nagel (St. Louis, MO: Concordia Publishing House, 1985), p. 126.

[3] Lucien Deiss, Springtime of the Liturgy, trans. Matthew J. O'Connell (Collegeville, MN: The Liturgical Press, 1979), p. 22. Deiss observes that similarities in the texts of the institution of the Lord's Supper cause scholars to put the accounts into two pairs, Matthew-Mark and Luke-Paul. Concerning the latter, he comments: "...it attests the usages of the Church of Antioch. Its Greek is of a better quality; but then Antiochene circles would quickly realize the necessity of an authentically Greek text for their liturgical celebrations." Joachim Jeremias observes: "In Paul . . . the very first words are liturgical, for the phrase 'the Lord Jesus' is not used in narrative; it is therefore not found in any of the gospels, but rather belongs to the liturgical formulae ... The concise 'in the same way also the cup', with which Paul introduces the word over the cup, sounds like an instruction for the celebrant . . ." Joachim Jeremias, The Eucharistic Words of Jesus, trans. Norman Perrin (Philadelphia, PA: Fortress Press, 1986), pp. 112-113.

[4] Hans Lietzmann, Mass and the Lord's Supper, trans. Dorothea H. G. Reeve (Leiden: E. J. Brill, 1979), pp. 207-208. Lietzmann's theory is that there were two prevalent understandings of the Lord's Supper in first century Christendom, the Petrine (Jerusalem) view that it was a fellowship meal, and the Pauline (realist) view that the bread was actually the atoning body of Christ (see pp. 204-208). It is beyond the scope of this study to engage at length Lietzmann's basic thesis. It should be noted, however, that the Church received all four accounts of the Last Supper, and the fundamental difference in theology alleged by Lietzmann to be presented by those accounts must not have been recognized by the Church.

[5] Sasse, pp. 49-54.

[6] Büchsel, παράδοσις, TDNT, 2:172

[7] Peter Bläser et al., Amt und Eucharistie (Paderborn: Verlag Bonifacius-Druckerei, 1973). See especially pp. 40-47, the section entitled "Die Verbindung von Amt und Eucharistie im Neuen Testament."

[8] Bläser, p. 44. These same passages are cited by Jeremias, p. 249.

54

[9] TWOT, 2:701.

[10] Braun, ποιεω, TDNT 6:483.

[11] For a thoroughgoing documentation of the evidence that the Last Supper was in fact a Passover meal, see Jeremias, pp. 41-88, and above, Chapter II, note 1.

[12] Ibid., p. 50.

[13] Ibid., p. 55-56.

[14] Bläser, pp. 45-46.

[15] For example, R. C. D. Jasper and G. J. Cuming, Prayers of the Eucharist: Early and reformed, 3rd rev. ed. (New York: Pueblo Publishing Co., 1987), p. 18; Hermann Sasse, We Confess the Sacraments, p. 84; Jeremias, pp. 118-121. See also 1 Cor. 10:16.

PART II:

THE TESTIMONY OF SELECTED EARLY
CHURCH FATHERS AND CHURCH
ORDERS

CHAPTER V

LITURGICAL REFERENCES IN CLEMENT OF ROME, IGNATIUS, AND JUSTIN MARTYR

L ittle exists in the way of written records concerning the liturgical life of the Church in the first two centuries beyond that which is found in Scripture itself. There is the short document called the *Didache*, a church order of sorts, the date of which is disputed, but certainly belonging to one of the first two centuries. However, we have no complete text of an ordinary Sunday liturgy for almost 300 years. Apparently the Christians of that day were familiar enough with the divine service that they felt no need to produce a written record of it, and what is known by heart has its own tenacity. If written records were produced, they are lost. This makes difficult an investigation into the liturgical relation of the Office of the Holy Ministry to the celebration of the Lord's Supper in these early years of the Church. One may compensate for this general absence of the texts of liturgies and church orders by examining the writings of the earliest church fathers for comments pertinent to the subject. Three church fathers that provide useful insight into the relation of office and celebration of the Lord's Supper at the end of the first and the beginning of the second centuries are Clement, Ignatius, and Justin Martyr. Their writings will now be considered.

Clement

In A.D. 95 or 96,[1] a letter was written by Clement of Rome to the church in Corinth. It contains several statements which pertain to the present enquiry. Clement draws a clear distinction between clergy and laity:

> Now the offerings and the ministrations [λειτουργιας] He commanded to be performed with care, and not to be done rashly or in disorder, but at fixed times and seasons. And where and by whom He would have them performed, He Himself fixed by His supreme will: that all things be done with piety according to His good pleasure might be acceptable to His will. They therefore that make their offerings at the appointed seasons are acceptable and blessed: for while they follow the institutions of the Master they cannot go wrong. For unto the high-priest [αρχιερει] his proper services [ιδιαι λειτουργιαι] have been assigned, and to the priests [ιθερευσιν] their proper office [ιδιος τοπος] is appointed, and upon the levites [λευιταις] their proper ministrations [ιδιαι διακονιαι] are laid. The layman is bound by the layman's ordinances.[2]

A Christian does not rebel against those whom the Lord has "fixed by His supreme will" to be ministers in His Church; faith does not seek to improve upon that which has been given to it by Christ. Further, it is clear that novelties were not to be introduced. It is as "the institutions of the Master" are followed that "they cannot go wrong." Thus Clement confesses the apostolic παραδοσις (see Chapter IV).

It is noteworthy that Clement employs the terms "high-priest," "priest," and "levite" to describe the various services of the clergy. He speaks of these in language taken from the ministry in the Old Testament. It is unclear to what extent the services, offices, and ministrations of the high-priest, priests, and deacons, respectively, are to be connected with the celebration of the Lord's Supper. Clement's next statement may well raise as many questions as it answers:

> Let each of you, brethren, in his own order give thanks [ευχαριστειτω] unto God, maintaining a good conscience and not transgressing the appointed rule [κανονα] of his service, but acting with all seemliness. Not in every place, brethren, are the continual daily sacrifices offered, or the freewill offerings, or the sin offerings and the trespass offerings, but in Jerusalem alone. And even there the offering is not made in every place, but before the sanctuary in the court of the altar; and this too through the High-Priest and the aforesaid ministers, after that the victim to be offered hath been inspected for blemishes. They therefore who do any thing contrary to the seemly ordinance of His will receive death as the penalty. Ye see, brethren, in proportion as greater knowledge hath been vouchsafed unto us, so much the more are we exposed to danger.[3]

The early Christians went to considerable lengths to protect the sacred formula of the Lord's Supper.[4] Is Clement here talking 'around' the Lord's Supper in the language of the Old Testament? The "give thanks" could refer to the "Eucharist" proper; "Jerusalem" could refer to the congregation's place of corporate worship; the "offerings" could refer to the elements of bread and wine; the "altar" to that area of the meeting place where the Lord's Supper was consecrated.

The reference to "death as the penalty" could refer to St. Paul's solemn warning in 1 Cor. 11:29-30. If this passage is understood this way, there would be a clear and exclusive connection between the Office of the Holy Ministry and the celebration of the Lord's Supper. If this explanation is seen as going beyond that which the evidence warrants, one may still say, at bare minimum, that Clement understood that certain functions, notably the offering of "sin offerings" and "trespass offerings," were to be done through those who held the Office of the Holy Ministry, and those who violated this rule risked calling divine judgment down upon themselves.

Ignatius

Ignatius was martyred as a result of a persecution that took place around A.D. 110. As he was being taken to his death, Ignatius wrote several letters, seven of which have survived. These provide a wealth of information concerning the Office of the Holy Ministry and liturgical practice at the dawn of the second century. This period of time was a critical point in the history of the Christian Church, as the last eye-witnesses of the Lord's earthly ministry were dying.[5] Ignatius' words were words of encouragement, admonishing unity and loyalty to the holy ministry.

> ... therefore was I forward to exhort you, that ye run in harmony with the mind of God: for Jesus Christ also, our inseparable life, is the mind of the Father, even as the bishops that are settled in the farthest parts of the earth are in the mind of Jesus Christ.
>
> So then it becometh you to run in harmony with the mind of the bishop; which thing also ye do. For your honorable presbytery, which is worthy of God, is attuned to the bishop, even as its strings to a lyre ...

Plainly therefore we ought to regard the bishop as the Lord Himself. ... ye do not so much as listen to anyone, if he speak of aught else [πλεον, i.e., "beyond"] save concerning Jesus Christ in truth.[6]

Regard for the bishop is thus being equated with regard for the Lord and His words. Yet the bishop is not to be heeded when he preaches something other than or beyond (πλεον) what is of Christ. Ignatius speaks in another letter of the authority entrusted by God to those who hold the Office of the Holy Ministry:

> ... I advise you, be zealous to do all things in godly concord, the bishop presiding [προκαθημενου] after the likeness of God and the presbyters after the likeness of the council of the apostles ... Let there be nothing among you which shall have power to divide you, but be united with the bishop and with them that preside [προκαθημενοις] over you ...
>
> Therefore as the Lord did nothing without the Father, [being united with Him], either by Himself or by the apostles, so neither do ye anything without the bishop and the presbyters.[7]

Statements enjoining obedience to the bishop as a vicar of Christ or of the Father, and referring to the presbytery as corresponding to the apostles may be found frequently in Ignatius' letters: "Be obedient to the bishop ... as Jesus Christ was to the Father ... ,"[8] "when ye are obedient to the bishop as to Jesus Christ, ... ye are living ... after Jesus Christ ... do nothing without the bishop, but be ye obedient also to the presbytery, ..."[9] "Do nothing without the bishop,"[10] "I am devoted to those who are subject to the bishop, the presbyters, the deacons."[11]

In view of all this it is inconceivable that there might be someone beside the bishops and the presbyters who was the celebrant at the Lord's Supper. A statement from Ignatius' letter to the Philadelphians in which the bishop, presbytery, and deacons are mentioned in connection with the Lord's Supper further suggests such a relation:

> Be ye careful therefore to observe one eucharist (for there is one flesh of our Lord Jesus Christ and one cup unto union in His blood; there is one altar, as there is one bishop, together with the presbytery and the deacons my fellow-servants), that whatsoever ye do, ye may do it after God (κατα Θεον).[12]

The statement mentioned above from the same letter, "Do nothing without the bishop," could hardly not apply to celebrations of the Lord's Supper. What the letter to the Philadelphians appears to imply, however, is explicitly stated in the letter to the Smyrnæans. Ignatius begins by refuting an apparently Docetic heresy, and then speaks, two paragraphs later, about the relation of the bishop to the celebration of the Lord's Supper:

> They abstain from the eucharist (thanksgiving) and prayer, because they allow not that the eucharist is the flesh of our Saviour Jesus Christ, which flesh suffered for our sins, and which the Father of His goodness raised up.
>
> ... Do ye all follow your bishop, as Jesus Christ followed the Father, and the presbytery as the apostles; and to the deacons pay respect, as to God's commandment. Let no man do aught of things pertaining to

the Church apart from the bishop. Let that be held a valid [βεβαια] eucharist which is under the bishop or one to whom he shall have committed it. Wheresoever the bishop shall appear, there let the people be; even as where Jesus may be, there is the universal Church.[13] It is not lawful apart from the bishop either to baptize or to hold a love-feast [αγαπην]; but whatsoever he shall approve, this is well pleasing also to God; that everything which ye do may be sure and valid [βεβαιον].[14]

At this point, then, there is an undeniable connection between the Office of the Holy Ministry and the celebration of the Lord's Supper, which is "the flesh of our Saviour Jesus Christ, which flesh suffered for our sins." The "or one to whom he shall have committed it" should probably be understood as taking into account presbyterial celebrations. In any case, a Lord's Supper which someone attempted to celebrate independently of the authority of the Office of the Holy Ministry—particularly the authority of the bishop—would not only have been considered a violation of good order; that which was purportedly celebrated could not be relied upon to be the sin-forgiving Lord's Supper! There is no certainty that a man whom the Lord of the Supper has not entrusted with the sin-forgiving office can celebrate the Lord's Supper. Lay celebration was not handed down from the Lord through His apostles.

Justin Martyr
Justin was born during the first decade of the second century, and was beheaded ca. A.D. 165. He was born a pagan, and associated himself with a number of pagan philosophical schools prior to his conversion to Christianity.[15] He is the

most important of the second century Greek apologists.[16]
He did most of his writing between A.D. 145 and 160.
Only two of his statements will be considered here. The
first comes from his *Dialogue with Trypho, a Jew*:

> For just as that Jesus (Joshua), called by the prophet
> a priest, evidently had on filthy garments because he
> is said to have taken a harlot for a wife, and is called a
> brand plucked out of the fire, because he had received
> remission of sins when the devil that resisted him
> was rebuked; even so we, who through the name of
> Jesus have believed as one man in God the Maker
> of all, have been stripped, through the name of His
> first-begotten Son, of the filthy garments, i.e. of our
> sins; and being vehemently inflamed by the word of
> His calling, we are the true high-priestly race of God
> [αρχι επαρικον το αληθινον γενος εσμεν του
> θεου], as even God Himself bears witness, saying
> that in every place among the Gentiles sacrifices are
> presented to Him well-pleasing and pure. Now God
> receives sacrifices from no one, except through His
> priests [ιερεων].
>
> Accordingly, God, anticipating all the sacrifices
> which we offer through this name, and which Jesus
> the Christ enjoined us to offer, i.e. in the Eucharist
> of the bread and the cup, and which are presented by
> Christians in all places throughout the world, bears
> witness that they are well-pleasing to Him.[17]

Of critical interest to this study is the line, "God receives
sacrifices from no one, except through His priests." The next
paragraph explains what those sacrifices are: those which
are offered "in the Eucharist of the bread and the cup." A

re-sacrificing of Christ is apparently not intended here; the sacrificial dimension of the Lord's Supper is the offering of the bread, the sacrifice of fine flour answering to Lev. 14:10.[18] This does not mean that he denies that the Lord's Supper is the body and blood of Christ (through whom one is "stripped of sins"), as may be seen clearly enough in his *First Apology*. However, he does limit the offering of sacrifice to God's priests. God will not receive them from anyone else. For Justin it follows that the Lord's Supper could only have God's priests as celebrants.

The question is, who are God's priests? Only a couple of lines earlier, Justin, speaking of all Christians, writes, "we are the true high-priestly race of God." The New Testament doctrine that God's chosen people are a "royal priesthood, a holy nation" (1 Peter 2:9) is not unique to the New Testament, but is rather a continuation of the Old Testament 'priesthood of all believers' (Ex. 19:6). The Old Testament 'priesthood of all believers' did not in any way take the place of having priests and Levites to serve in offering sacrifices and as liturgists in the divine services. Thus, it may be assumed that Justin was confessing to Trypho that, while Christians are God's true royal priesthood, God will still not receive their sacrifices except through the Office of the Holy Ministry, that is, through the priests. It has already been observed in the writings of Clement that the early Christians often referred to those who held the Office of the Holy Ministry in terms taken over from the Old Testament. One may thus conclude that when Justin speaks of God receiving sacrifices "from no one, except through His priests," the indication is that only one in the Office of the Holy Ministry is able to celebrate the Lord's Supper. That the "sacrifice" is offered through the priest does not in any way overthrow the fact that it is the offering of all of the believers, anymore than the dispensing of the forgiveness of sins by the hand of the priest changes the fact that Christ is the one doing the forgiving.[19]

Justin's *First Apology* sheds further light upon early Christian celebrations of the Lord's Supper. The letter is written as a defense of the practice of the Christian faith to a government which was hostile to it. It was written in Rome, and addressed to Emperor Antoninus Pius.[20] Justin apparently desired, among other things, to defend Christians against the charge of cannibalism.[21] In this work, Justin describes two celebrations of the Lord's Supper. The first follows a Baptism, the second is an account of the regular Sunday divine service. They are "the earliest surviving accounts of the eucharist."[22] Concerning the post-baptismal celebration of the Lord's Supper, Justin writes as follows:

> But we, after we have thus washed him who has been convinced and has assented to our teaching, bring him to the place where those who are called brethren are assembled, in order that we may offer hearty prayers in common for ourselves and for the baptized [illuminated] person, and for all others in every place, that we may be counted worthy, now that we have learned the truth, by our works also to be found good citizens and keepers of the commandments, so that we may be saved with an everlasting salvation. Having ended the prayers, we salute one another with a kiss. There is then brought to the president of the brethren [τω προεστωτι των αδελφων] bread and a cup of wine mixed with water; and he taking them, gives praise and glory to the Father of the universe, through the name of the Son and the Holy Ghost, and offers thanks at considerable length for being counted worthy to receive

these things at His hands. And when he has concluded the prayers and thanksgivings, all the people present express their assent by saying Amen ... And when the president [προεστωτος] has given thanks, and all the people have expressed their assent, those who are called by us deacons give to each of those present to partake of the bread and wine mixed with water over which the thanksgiving was pronounced, and to those who are absent when they carry away a portion.

And this food is called among us Ευχαριστια [the Eucharist], of which no one is allowed to partake but the man who believes that the things which we teach are true, and who has been washed with the washing that is for the remission of sins, and unto regeneration, and who is so living as Christ has enjoined. For not as common bread and common drink do we receive these; but in like manner as Jesus Christ our Saviour, having been made flesh by the word of God, had both flesh and blood for our salvation, so likewise have we been taught that the food which is blessed by the prayer of His word, and from which our blood and flesh by transmutation are nourished, is the flesh and blood of that Jesus who was made flesh. For the apostles, in the memoirs composed by them, which are called Gospels, have thus delivered unto us what was enjoined upon them; that Jesus took bread, and when He had given thanks, said, "This do ye in remembrance of me, this is my body"; and that, after the same manner, having taken the cup and given thanks, He said, "This is my blood"; and gave it to them alone.[23]

There is much that can be said concerning the information found in this passage about the relation of the celebrant to the celebration of the Lord's Supper. The celebrant is identified only as "τω προεστωτι των αδελφων," which, according to Marcus Dods, could be translated "that one of the brethren who was presiding."[24] Any pagan would have understood the term προεστως (president).[25] This is not surprising, however, as Justin was addressing a pagan, and it would have been pointless to use technical Christian terminology (such as "bishop" or "presbyter") which the recipient might not have understood. Because of the public nature of the ministry of the diaconate, taking the Lord's Supper to those who were sick or in prison, and so forth, Justin apparently assumed that his reader would be familiar with this term.[26]

What is to be made, then, of this "προεστως"? To begin to answer this, one notes that there is not a shred of evidence anywhere indicating that there was ever a Christian congregation that had a diaconate, but lacked a bishop. Ignatius insisted that the Lord's Supper be celebrated either by the bishop or by one whom the bishop had appointed, and it would be logical to assume that Justin was using the term "president" as a synonym for "bishop" which his reader would more readily understand. One statement in particular contrasts the 'president' with the 'people': ". . . when the president has given thanks, and all the people have expressed their assent . . ." The setting of these two terms over against each other would suggest that the 'president' held a position that distinguished him from the 'people.' The use of the term 'president' for a holder of the Office of the Holy Ministry accords fully with the statement made by St. Paul in 1 Tim. 5:17: "The elders who direct the affairs [οι καλως προεστωτες πρεσβυτεροι] of the Church well are worthy of double honor, especially those whose work is preaching and teaching."[27]

In conclusion, while it is not possible on the exclusive basis of the internal evidence to prove that the 'president' was a holder of the Office of the Holy Ministry, the conclusion that he was in fact such an office-holder has more to say for it than the suggestion that he might not have been. He was clearly acknowledged as doing something which the people did not do. The discussion of the Sunday celebration adds little to this inquiry:

> And on the day called Sunday, all who live in cities or in the country gather together to one place, and the memoirs of the apostles or the writings of the prophets are read, as long as time permits; then, when the reader has ceased, the president verbally instructs, and exhorts to the imitation of these good things. Then we all rise together and pray, and, as we before said, when our prayer is ended, bread and wine and water are brought, and the president [προεστως] in like manner offers prayers and thanksgivings, according to his ability, and the people assent, saying Amen; and there is a distribution to each, and a participation of that over which thanks have been given, and to those who are absent a portion is sent by the deacons.[28]

The 'president' is responsible for giving instruction and exhortation to the people. It is he who offers the prayers and thanksgivings. Again, he is seen as distinct from the people, who assent to what he does with their "Amen." Again deacons are mentioned, and again the curious absence of any reference to a bishop would cause one to suspect that the president is in the Office of the Holy Ministry. The description of the president's duties (instructing, exhorting, saying particular prayers) further confirms this. One may acknowledge that the text itself does not use some of the customary terms. This is not surprising, however, as he is writing to the pagan emperor. Nevertheless, it is natural to read it in harmony with the additional witness of such sources as Ignatius and 1 Tim. 5:17.

Examined together, these three church fathers produce a clear picture of the relation between the Office of the Holy Ministry and the celebration of the Lord's Supper. Unless it is assumed that Ignatius and Justin simply contradict one another, it would appear that an office-holder was the president at the divine service. Clement emphasizes the distinction between clergy and laity, and employs vocabulary demonstrative of the continuity he sees between the Office of the Holy Ministry in the Old Testament and that of the New Testament. He emphasizes that what the Lord has instituted for the forgiveness of sins is certain not to go wrong as His institutions are followed. Particularly in Ignatius, the Lord's Supper is to be celebrated by someone who holds the office. To act contrary to this would be more than just a violation of good order. The Lord has entrusted His Supper to those who hold the office. In order for the forgiveness of sins dispensed in the Lord's Supper to be reliable, it must necessarily be celebrated by one to whom the Lord has entrusted its celebration. To this, these three fathers of the Church bear witness.

Notes:

[1] Georges Blond, *Clement of Rome*, in The Eucharist of the Early Christians, trans. Matthew J. O'Connell (New York: Pueblo Publishing Company, 1978), p. 24.

[2] Clement of Rome, *Corinthians 40*, in J. B. Lightfoot and J. R, Harmer, eds., The Apostolic Fathers (Grand Rapids, MI: Baker Book House, 1988), p.

74. For the Greek, see pp. 26-27.

[3] Ibid., 41, Greek: p. 27, English: pp. 74-75.

[4] For a scholarly discussion of this topic, together with its application to the apparent absence of an account of the institution of the Lord's Supper in the Gospel according to St. John, see Joachim Jeremias, The Eucharistic Words of Jesus, trans. Norman Perrin (Philadelphia: Fortress Press, 1986), pp. 132-137.

[5] Raymond Johanny, Ignatius of Antioch, in The Eucharist of the Early Christians, pp. 48-49.

[6] Ignatius, Ephesians 3, 4, 6. Cited by Lightfoot, English: pp. 138-139, Greek: pp. 106-107. See Matt. 10:40; 21:33-43; Mark 12:1-12; Luke 20:9-19; John 13:20.

[7] Ignatius, Magnesians 6, 7; in Lightfoot, English: p. 144, Greek: p. 113.

[8] Ibid., English: p. 146, Greek: p. 115.

[9] Ignatius, Trallians 2; in Lightfoot, English: p. 147, Greek: p. 116. See also sections 3, 7, 12.

[10] Ignatius, Philadelphians 7; in Lightfoot, English: p. 155, Greek: p. 125.

[11] Ignatius, To Polycarp 6; in Lightfoot, English: p. 161, Greek: p. 133.

[12] Ignatius, Philadelphians 4; in Lightfoot, English: p. 154, Greek: p. 124. Ignatius makes similar comments in his letter Ephesians 20.2.

[13] It was seen above that clergy is clergy as it is Christ's clergy. Here one sees that the same principle applies to the Church: Church is Church as it is Christ's Church.

[14] Ignatius, Smyrnæans 6-8; in Lightfoot, English: p. 158, Greek: pp. 129-130. The translation of βεβαιον as "valid" is less than ideal, as it would tend to impose an anachronistic Augustinian distinction between a "valid" and an "effective" Lord's Supper. BAGD, p. 138, offers the following definition: "Of the eucharist dependable in its effect, or valid ISm 8:1." Again, however, the term "valid" should not be understood in an Augustinian sense, but as synonymous with reliable, dependable, or certain. This same Greek verb is used in 1 Cor. 1:6 and 1:8 to mean confirmed, strong, unshaken.

[15] William A. Jurgens, The Faith of the Early Fathers, vol. 1 (Collegeville, MN: The Liturgical Press, 1970), p. 50.

[16] Johannes Quasten, Patrology, vol. 1 (Westminster, MD: The Newman Press, 1951), p. 196.

[17] Justin Martyr, Dialogue with Trypho 116-117. Translation by G. Reith, cited in Alexander Roberts and James Donaldson, eds., Ante-Nicene Christian Library, (Edinburgh: T. and T. Clark, 1867), vol. 2, pp. 245-246. (Hereafter ANCL). For the Greek text and a Latin translation, see J. P. Migne, ed., Patrologiæ Cursus Completus, Series Græca, (Paris, 1857-1866), vol. 6, pp. 743-746. (Hereafter MPG).

[18] Maurice Jourjon, Justin, in The Eucharist of the Early Christians, p. 80.

[19] Ibid., p. 80.

[20] Quasten, p. 199.

72

[21] R. C. D. Jasper and G. J. Cuming, Prayers of the Eucharist: Early and reformed, 3rd rev. ed. (New York: Pueblo Publishing Co., 1987), p. 26. Hermann Sasse notes that "the reproach of 'Thyestian meals,' that is, cultic cannibalism, . . . accompanied the ancient church through the whole period of persecution," on which basis he concludes that the Lord's Supper is not understood in the way of the mystery religions, with which ancient heathenism would have been familiar and to which they would not have reacted so negatively. Hermann Sasse, We Confess the Sacraments, trans. Norman Nagel (St. Louis, MO: Concordia Publishing House, 1985), p. 84.

[22] Ibid., p. 25.

[23] Justin Martyr, First Apology.65-66. Translated by Marcus Dods, cited in Roberts, ANCL, pp. 63-65. For the Greek and a Latin translation, see MPG 6:427-430.

[24] Roberts, ANCL, p. 63, note 4.

[25] Maurice Jourjon, Justin, in The Eucharist of the Early Christians, p. 74.

[26] Ibid., p. 75.

[27] See in this regard Reicke, προιστημι, in TDNT 6:702.

[28] Justin Martyr, First Apology.67. Cited in Roberts, ANCL, p. 65. For the Greek and a Latin translation, see MPG 6:429-430.

CHAPTER VI

THE DIDACHE (Διδαχη)

The *Didache* is the earliest example of an eccesiastical document resembling a church order that is presently known. R. C. D. Jasper and G. J. Cuming, on the basis of some apparently pre-Matthean language contained in the document, suggest the possibility of dating it as early as A.D. 60.[1] William A. Jurgens advances the following results of the "best current scholarship" concerning the *Didache*:

> The part of the *Didache* comprising Ch. 1, V. 1-3a and Chs. 2, V. 2 through the end of Ch. 6 is originally a Jewish work for the instruction of gentile proselytes to Judaism. This Jewish *Grundschrift*, possibly a work of Essene origin, may be referred to as the *Two Ways Document* or the *Urdidache*. In Syria not later than A. D. 160 and perhaps about A. D. 140, the *Two Ways Document* found entrance to Christian circles. The parts comprising Ch. 1, V. 3b through Ch. 2, V. 1, and Ch. 7, V. 1 to the end (Ch. 16, V. 8) were added by a Christian, thus producing the *Didache* as we have it now, a work for the instruction of catechumens.[2]

Varying theories of both composition and date of origin have been proposed, and an examination of all of these theories is not possible here.[3] In any case, a date ca. A.D. 100 is suggested, and greater precision is probably not possible. This source critical information is useful in understanding the structure of the document. Nevertheless, the entire document was received by some Christian community, and no part may be considered less indicative of early Christian thought than another. The very probability that it has been edited only further suggests that it has been modified to accurately reflect the confession of the catholic faith at that time.

> In regard to the Eucharist[4]—you shall give thanks thus: First, in regard to the cup:—We give you thanks, our Father, for the holy vine of David your son, which you have made known to us through Jesus your Son. Glory be to you forever. In regard to the broken bread:—We give you thanks, our Father, for the life and knowledge which you have made known to us through Jesus your Son. Glory be to you forever. As this broken bread was scattered on the mountains, but brought together was made one, so gather your Church from the ends of the earth into your kingdom. For yours is the glory and the power through Jesus Christ forever. Let no one eat or drink of the Eucharist with you except those who have been baptized in the name of the Lord; for it was in reference to this that the Lord said: "Do not give that which is holy to dogs."[5]

It is unclear whether this describes a celebration of the Lord's Supper, or if an *agape* (love feast) is being described here. Gregory Dix seems quite certain that this is simply an *agape*,[6] while Jasper and Cuming present some of the arguments advanced on both sides of the debate, and note that there is no agreement on this matter, as it pertains to either chapter 9 (above) or chapter 10 (below).[7] That admission to this meal was restricted suggests that some supervision must have been exercised over it, and supervision implies a supervisor. Nowhere is an allusion made to this supervisor, however, and since it is not even possible to finally state that a Lord's Supper is being discussed, it is not possible to speak clearly of a connection between the Office of the Holy Ministry and the celebration of the Lord's Supper on the basis of this evidence. Chapter 10 adds little to the inquiry:

> After you have eaten your fill, give thanks thus: We thank you, holy Father, for your holy name, which you have caused to dwell in our hearts; and for the knowledge and faith and immortality which you have made known to us through Jesus your Son. Glory be to you forever. You, almighty Master, have created all things for your name's sake, and have given food and drink to men for their enjoyment, so that they might return thanks to you. Upon us, however, you have bestowed spiritual food and drink, and eternal life through your Servant. Above all we give you thanks, because you are mighty. Glory be to you forever.
>
> Remember, O Lord, your Church. Deliver it from every evil and perfect it in your love. Gather it from the four winds, sanctified for your kingdom, which you have prepared for it. For yours is the power and the glory forever. Let grace come, and let this world pass away. Osanna to the God of David. If anyone is holy, let him come; if anyone is not, let him repent. Marana Tha. Amen. But allow the prophets to give thanks as they will.[8]

Joachim Jeremias argues that these two chapters pertain to an *agape*, which was then followed by a celebration of the Lord's Supper. The sentence, "If anyone is holy, let him come; if anyone is not, let him repent," has the sound of an invitation, and would not make sense if understood strictly as a statement made after the meal to which they pertained was already concluded. Instead, Jeremias sees these as being the preface to a post-*agape* celebration of the Lord's Supper.[9] One would then understand the final sentence of chapter 10 to mandate allowing "the prophets" to celebrate the Lord's Supper, a position also held by Johannes Quasten.[10] The internal evidence of these two chapters is inconclusive. Bringing external evidence to bear, it is apparent from the statements of Ignatius that, whether a Lord's Supper, an *agape*, or both is here described, it was to be done under the authority of the bishop.

While chapters 9 and 10 remain matters of dispute, chapter 14 is widely acknowledged to refer to the Lord's Supper:

> On the Lord's Day gather together, break bread and give thanks, after confessing your transgressions so that your sacrifice may be pure. Let no one who has a quarrel with his neighbor join you until he is reconciled, lest your sacrifice be defiled. For this is that which was proclaimed by the Lord: "In every place and time let there be offered to Me a clean sacrifice. For I am a Great King," says the Lord, "and My name is wonderful among the gentiles."[11]

It is noted in passing that the reference to "sacrifice" probably does not refer to a sacrificing of the body and blood of the Lord (as with the "unbloody sacrifice" found in the *Apostolic Constitutions*). Rather, it refers to the act of giving thanks.[12] Thus, one may not connect the Office of the Holy Ministry with the celebration of the Lord's Supper at this point by appealing to a sacrificial dynamic of the office. Clearly, if bread is to be broken, someone must break it. Nevertheless, no one in particular is mentioned in this regard. It must be noted that this is far from being a complete text of the divine service. The words of consecration are not even mentioned. This hardly justifies an *argumentum a silentio* that they were not in fact spoken. One cannot know that the Lord's Supper is being celebrated unless the Lord's words are put upon it. In any case, neither the words, nor the identity of the one entrusted with speaking them, are mentioned here. This may not be surprising in "a work for the instruction of catechumens." The Office of the Holy Ministry was presupposed by the author of the *Didache*. The next chapter provides for men to be placed into that office:

> Elect for yourselves, therefore, bishops and deacons worthy of the Lord, humble men and not lovers of money, truthful and proven; for they also serve [λει–τουργουσι] you in the ministry [λειτουργιαν] of the prophets and teachers. Do not, therefore, despise them; for they are your honorable men, together with the prophets and teachers. Correct one another, not in anger but in peace, as you find it in the gospel; and let no one speak with you who has done a wrong to his neighbor, nor let him hear, until he repents. Your prayers and your alms and all your acts you shall perform as you find in the gospel of our Lord.[13]

The absence of any reference to presbyters is striking, and implies that this church order is the product of a day in which the Office of the Holy Ministry had not yet been divided into the superior rank of bishop and the subordinate rank of presbyter, or at least the distinctions between them were not as sharp. A "monarchial episcopate" is not indicated, and Quasten observes that, in the *Didache*, "the prophets still celebrate the eucharist, and it is necessary to stress that the actual liturgical ministers, the bishops and deacons, are entitled to no less honor and respect on the part of the faithful."[14] If one understands the Greek term λειτουργειν in a specifically cultic ("liturgical") way, it would be logical to assume that the bishop would be the liturgical celebrant of the Lord's Supper. Whether or not the Greek term should be understood this way, however, is open to question.[15] One further note of caution in finding a connection between the Office of the Holy Ministry and the celebration of the Lord's Supper in *Didache* 15 is sounded by Willy Rordorf, who bluntly asserts that "chapter 15 is certainly a later addition."[16]

To summarize concerning the Didache, it was certainly not intended to be an exhaustive instruction manual for the order of a divine service. The words of consecration and the forgiveness of sins are not even mentioned, nor is the person who is entrusted with speaking them ever specified. It is clear that the Office of the Holy Ministry served an important role, as provisions are made for appointing bishops and deacons. That no mention is made of presbyters suggests that a distinction was not yet being made between two ranks of office-holders. The duties of a bishop are mentioned nowhere, so one must turn to the writings of Scripture and the early church fathers to establish that these duties included, along with the forgiving and retaining of sins, the celebration of the Lord's Supper.

Notes:
[1] R. C. D. Jasper and G. J. Cuming, <u>Prayers of the Eucharist: Early and reformed</u>, 3rd rev. ed. (New York: Pueblo Publishing Co., 1987), p. 20.
[2] William A. Jurgens, <u>The Faith of the Early Fathers</u>, vol. 1 (Collegeville,

MN: The Liturgical Press, 1970), p. 1. See also in this regard Rudolph Stählin, "Die Geschichte des christlichen Gottesdienstes von der Urkirche bis zur Gaegenwart," in Karl Ferdinand Müller and Walter Blankenburg, eds., Leiturgia, vol. 1 (Kassel: Johannes Stauda Verlag, 1954), p. 16: "Sie ist ein „Laienkatechismus", für die Gemeinde bestimmt und ihre Katecheten, so daß man in ihr keine „Agende" für die Hand des Bischofs erwarten darf."

[3] For a summary of the various theories, see Cheslyn Jones, Geoffrey Wainwright, and Edward Yarnold, eds., The Study of the Liturgy (New York: Oxford University Press, 1978), pp. 55-56. See also Willy Rordorf, "The Didache," in The Eucharist of the Early Christians, trans. Matthew J. O'Connell (New York: Pueblo Publishing Company, 1978), pp. 1-2.

[4] The Greek word here, ευχαριστιας, may simply be translated "thanksgiving," and need not therefore be understood as a technical designation of the Lord's Supper. See also Willy Rordorf, The Didache, in The Eucharist of the Early Christians, p. 8.

[5] Didache 9:1-5, as cited in William A. Jurgens, The Faith of the Early Fathers, vol. 1 (Collegeville, MN: The Liturgical Press, 1970), p. 3. For the Greek text, see J. B. Lightfoot and J. R. Harmer, eds., The Apostolic Fathers (Grand Rapids, MI: Baker Book House, 1988), p. 221.

[6] Gregory Dix, The Shape of the Liturgy (London: Dacre Press, 1960), pp. 90-93.

[7] Jasper and Cuming, pp. 20-21.

[8] Didache 10:1-7, as cited in Jurgens, p. 3. For the Greek text, see Lightfoot, pp. 221-222.

[9] Joachim Jeremias, The Eucharistic Words of Jesus, trans. Norman Perrin (Philadelphia: Fortress Press, 1986), p. 118.

[10] Johannes Quasten, Patrology, vol. 1 (Westminster, MD: The Newman Press, 1951), pp. 33-34. Quasten is quite specific concerning chapters 9 and 10: "Not only numerous other indications but especially the context warrants the assumption that these prescriptions were intended to regulate the First Communion of the newly baptized on Easter eve. The ordinary Eucharistic service held on Sundays is described in chapter 14 . . ."

[11] Didache 14:1-3, as cited in Jurgens, p. 4. For the Greek text, see Lightfoot, pp. 223f.

[12] Willy Rordorf, The Didache, in The Eucharist of the Early Christians, p. 17.

[13] Didache 15:1-4, as cited in Jurgens, p. 4. For the Greek text, see Lightfoot, p. 224.

[14] Quasten, p. 37.

[15] Strathmann: "It should never be forgotten that in the first instance λει–τουργειν, λειτουργγια simply denotes service, the pious service which is rendered to God . . . and also to the community (. . . Did., 15, 1). But comparison with the relations of the OT, and the contrast between the priesthood and the [laity] in 1 Cl., suggest the beginnings of an approximation of the terms for Christian

office to those for the OT priesthood, and this was bound to exert an influence on the history of the meaning of λειτουργειν, λειτουργια.... The final result . .. was a thoroughgoing transfer of the OT concept of the priest to the Christian clergy." Strathmann, λειτουργεω, in <u>TDNT</u> 4:228-229.

[16] Rordorf, *The Didache*, in <u>The Eucharist of the Early Christians</u>, p. 17.

CHAPTER VII

THE DIDASCALIA (Διδασκαλια)

The date of the origin of the *Didascalia* has not been established with precision. R. H. Connolly appears to be convinced that it is not possible to be more specific than to say that it was written in the third century.[1] Marcel Metzger asserts that it was written during the first half of that century, "very probably in the first decades of it." He further indicates that the author was a bishop from Syria.[2]

Although the *Didascalia* was originally written in Greek, only fragments of the work have been preserved in that language.[3] It has been preserved "thanks solely to an avid commitment unparalled [sic] in the entire history of ancient Christian literature, namely, the determined effort of the Syrians to translate almost everything on which they could lay their hands into their own language."[4] The Syriac is found in four principle codices: Sangermanensis, Harrisianus, Borgianus, and Cantabrigiensis.[5] A large portion of the work is also preserved in the Latin Verona fragments.[6]

References in the *Didascalia* to the ordination of bishops and presbyters provide for their selection by "all the people,"[7] but a specific rite of ordination is not given, and little more is said in these references concerning the Office of the Holy Ministry other than to discuss the (largely moral) qualifications of those men who are to serve in this capacity. There are, however, several other references which pertain to this study. The first is an admonition to the laity:

But do you honour the bishops, who have loosed you from sins, who by the water regenerated you, who filled you with the Holy Spirit, who reared you with the word as with milk, who bred you up with doctrine, who confirmed you with admonition, and made you partake of the holy Eucharist of God, and made you partakers and joint heirs of the promise of God.[8]

From this statement the responsibilities of a bishop in the third century may be seen: he absolved, baptized, admonished, instructed, and celebrated the Lord's Supper. In short, the bishop appears to have been the congregation's steward of 'the means of grace'; that is, he was entrusted with the administration of those things through which forgiveness was dispensed. While there is much that could be said about this passage, of primary importance to this study is that the bishop is the one credited with making the people partakers of the Lord's Supper. The *Didascalia*, then, clearly connects the Office of the Holy Ministry, the holders of which office "have loosed you from sins," with the celebration of the Lord's Supper. Further insight into the bishop's role as celebrant may be gained from the following statement:

But if a presbyter should come from another congregation, do you the presbyters receive him with fellowship into your place. And if it be a bishop, let him sit with the bishop; and let him accord him the honour of his rank, even as himself. And do thou, O bishop, invite him to discourse to thy people; for the exhortation and admonition of strangers is very profitable, especially as it is written: *There is no prophet that is acceptable in his own place.* And when you offer the oblation, let him speak. But if he is wise and gives the honour to thee, and is unwilling to offer, at least let him speak over the cup.[9]

As a courtesy to a visiting bishop, the bishop of the host congregation was enjoined to offer to the visiting bishop the honor of being the celebrant. If the visiting bishop were equally courteous and humble, that offer would be declined. At that point, the host bishop would act as the primary celebrant by speaking the words of consecration over the bread, but he was apparently expected to insist that the visiting bishop speak the consecratory words over the cup! In the *Didascalia*, the important thing in the celebration of the Lord's Supper was not the man (or the men) who did it, but the office they held. Later, when the *Apostolic Constitutions* were compiled, the practice of a dual presidency at the celebration of the Lord's Supper was apparently no longer known (see below).

By the time the *Didascalia* was written, the Office of the Holy Ministry had been clearly divided between bishops as superiors and presbyters as subordinate to them. No comment is made about the possibility of presbyterial celebration. The author appears to have presupposed that there would be a sufficient number of bishops to render a consideration of presbyterial celebration unnecessary.

Notes:
[1] R. H. Connolly, ed., *Didascalia Apostolorum* (Oxford: The Clarendon Press, 1929), pp. lxxxix-xc.
[2] Marcel Metzger, "The Didascalia and Constitutiones Apostolorum," in The Eucharist of the Early Christians, trans. Matthew J. O'Connell (New York: Pueblo Publishing Company, 1978), p. 194.
[3] Arthur Vööbus, The Didascalia Apostolorum in Syriac, vol. 1, tome 176 (Louvain: Corpus Scriptorum Christianorum Orientalum, 1979), p. 23.
[4] Ibid., p. 25. Vööbus has edited a critical Syriac text of this work in two

84

volumes. They are The Didascalia Apostolorum in Syriac, Chapters I-X, tome 175, edited by Arthur Vööbus (Louvain, Belgium: Corpus Scriptorum Christianorum Orientalum, 1979), and The Didascalia Apostolorum in Syriac, Chapters XI-XXVI, tome 179, edited by Arthur Vööbus (Louvain, Belgium: Corpus Scriptorum Christianorum Orientalum, 1979).

[5] Connolly, Didascalia, pp. xi-xviii. These pages also contain information about each of these codices, should this be desired.

[6] Ibid., pp. xviii-xx.

[7] Didascalia Apostolorum, 3:8b. Horae Semiticae No. II, The Didascalia Apostolorum in English, trans. Margaret Dunlop Gibson (London: C. J. Clay and Sons, 1903), pp. 10-11. This citation is found in the codex Harrisianus manuscript (see p. v), but not in the codex Sangermanensis.

[8] Didascalia Apostolorum, 9:33, in Connolly, Didascalia, p. 94.

[9] Ibid., 12:58. The Latin of the Verona fragments reads as follows: "Si autem praesbyter de ecclesia parrociae uenerit, suscipite eum, praesbyteri, communiter in loco uestro. Et si episcopus aduenerit, cum episcopo sedeat, eundem honorem ab eo recipiens. Et petes eum tu, episcope, ut adloquatur plebem tuam, quoniam peregrinus, cum adloquium dat, deiubat populum; scriptum est enim: Nullus propheta susceptus est in patria sua. Et in gratia agenda ipse dicat. Si autem, cum sit prudens et honorem tibi reseruans, non uelit, super calicem dicat." Connolly, Didascalia, pp. 120-123.

CHAPTER VIII

THE APOSTOLIC TRADITION (Ἀποστολικη παραδοσις) OF HIPPOLYTUS

The *Apostolic Tradition* was apparently written around A.D. 215, which would make it roughly contemporaneous with the *Didascalia*. The Greek title[1] of the work is found among other works of Hippolytus on his statue, and most scholars agree that the title belongs to the work reviewed here.[2] Portions of the Greek text are preserved, probably with some modification, in the *Epitome of the Apostolic Constitutions*.[3] The work is extant in Arabic, Coptic, Ethiopic and Latin, as well as in several adaptations.[4] The reasons for this are presented by Joseph A. Jungmann:

> The work was probably completed about 215, before the schism which broke out when Callistus was chosen pope. The division that followed, together with the fact that the work was done in Greek, explains why the *Apostolic Tradition*, like so many of the writings of Hippolytus, was almost entirely forgotten in Rome and in the West, while in the Orient, in Egypt as well as in Syria, precisely because it claimed to present the apostolic tradition and because it came from Rome, it had a tremendous success. And that explains why, except for a few tiny fragments, it has survived not in the original text, but in translation—in Coptic, Arabic, Ethiopian and partly in Syrian.[5]

Thus, while having had a somewhat limited influence upon the Church in the West, its lasting influence upon the liturgical confession of the Church in the East can hardly be overstated. In Ethiopia it remains to this day, entitled "Anaphora of the Apostles."[6]

This having been noted, a word of caution is in order regarding the extent to which one treats this liturgy as representative of the practice of the Church in general at the dawn of the third century. Paul F. Bradshaw writes,

> This early Church order, however, needs to be treated with greater caution than it has generally received. Although it is usually dated c. A.D. 215 and regarded as providing reliable information about the life and liturgical activity of the Church in Rome at this period, a few scholars entertain doubts .... In any case, it is dangerous to draw the conclusion that other Christian communities in the third century would necessarily have followed a similar practice to that described here. Furthermore, since the Greek original of the document has not survived, except in the form of a few isolated fragments, it has to be reconstructed from an extant Latin translation and from later Coptic, Arabic, and Ethiopic versions, as well as from the use made of it by compilers of later Church orders, which increases the difficulty of determining exactly what the author wrote.[7]

One may summarize the foregoing by saying that while that which one finds recorded in the *Apostolic Tradition* of Hippolytus does not necessarily represent the practice of the Church in all places at the time of his writings, he was certainly no innovator. Further, precisely to the extent that his liturgical writings do not reflect the general practice of the Church catholic at the beginning of the third century but later came to be generally received, the influence of this document upon further liturgical development may be noted.[8]

The text begins by providing a rite for the ordination of a bishop. The introductory paragraph includes the following statement:

> And we address the churches, so that they who have been well trained, may, by our instruction, hold fast that tradition which has continued up to now and, knowing it well, may be strengthened. This is needful, because of that lapse or error which recently occurred through ignorance, and because of ignorant men . . .[9]

R. C. D. Jasper and G. J. Cuming indicate that the reference to "that tradition which has continued up to now" suggest that the contents reflect the liturgical practice of the Church in Rome for the preceding fifty years.[10] This statement, and the title of the work itself, are certainly reflective of Hippolytus' desire to be "holding to the teachings [traditions] just as I [the Apostle Paul] passed them on to you" (1 Cor. 11:2). Elsewhere in his writings, Hippolytus clearly treats novelties as being *ipso facto* heretical.[11] In any case, he certainly does not undertake to introduce something new. Rather, he is reacting precisely against the introduction of what he perceives to be novelties, as his opening paragraph indicates.[12]

Hippolytus' work is particularly valuable to this study, as it contains descriptions of two celebrations of the Lord's Supper, one following a Baptism and the other following an ordination. The service of ordination is itself most noteworthy:

Let the bishop be ordained after he has been chosen by all the people. When he has been named and shall please all, let him, with the presbytery and such bishops as may be present, assemble with the people on a Sunday. While all give their consent, the bishops shall lay their hands upon him, and the presbytery shall stand by in silence. All indeed shall keep silent, praying in their heart for the descent of the Spirit. Then one of the bishops who are present shall, at the request of all, lay his hand on him who is ordained bishop, and shall pray as follows, saying:

God and Father of our Lord Jesus Christ, Father of mercies and God of all comfort, who dwellest on high yet hast respect to the lowly, who knowest all things before they come to pass. Thou hast appointed the borders of thy church by thy grace, predestinating from the beginning the righteous race of Abraham. And making them princes and priests, and leaving not thy sanctuary without a ministry, thou hast from the beginning of the world been pleased to be glorified among those whom thou hast chosen. Pour forth now that power, which is thine, of thy royal Spirit, which through thy beloved son Jesus Christ thou gavest to thy holy apostles, who established the church in every place, the church which thou hast sanctified unto unceasing glory and praise of thy name. Thou who knowest the hearts of all, grant to this thy servant, whom thou hast chosen to be bishop, [to feed thy holy flock][13] and to serve as thy high priest without blame, ministering night and day, to propitiate thy countenance without ceasing and to offer thee the gifts of thy holy church.

And by the Spirit of high-priesthood to have authority to remit sins according to thy commandment,[14] to assign the lots according to thy precept, to loose every bond according to the authority which thou gavest to thy holy apostles, and to please thee in meekness and purity of heart, offering to thee an odour of sweet savour. Through thy Servant Jesus Christ our Lord, through whom be to thee glory, might, honour, with [the] Holy Spirit in [the] holy church, both now and always and world without end. Amen.[15]

In this ordination, the bishop is entrusted, "by the Spirit" with the "authority to remit sins" and "to loose every bond." Ordination consists in the bestowing of this authority upon a man; holding the Office of the Holy Ministry consists in being a man entrusted with this authority. The "authority to remit sins" is certainly inclusive of the authority to celebrate the Lord's Supper "for the forgiveness of sins," which the newly ordained bishop proceeds immediately to do. Particularly noteworthy are the very first words which the congregation speaks to him subsequent to his ordination:

And when he is made bishop, all shall offer him the kiss of peace, for he has been made worthy. To him then the deacons shall bring the offering, and he, laying his hand upon it, with all the presbytery, shall say as the thanksgiving:
The Lord be with you.
And all shall say
And with thy spirit.
Lift up your hearts.
We lift them up unto the Lord.
Let us give thanks to the Lord.

It is meet and right.

And then he shall proceed immediately:[16]

There follows here a prayer of consecration over
the elements, which incorporates the words of institution.
According to the church order of Hippolytus, then, the very
first thing that a bishop did after he had been ordained was
celebrate the Lord's Supper. The very first words spoken to
him by the congregation were "and with thy spirit."[17] This can
only be a reference to the Spirit which he had just received
in his ordination, that Spirit for the descent of Whom the
presbyters and the whole congregation were instructed to
pray silently prior to the ordination. As such, the liturgy
made no allowances for the possibility that one who was not
ordained would celebrate the Lord's Supper—no allowances
were made for such a possibility because it simply was not
possible. Only one who had been given the Spirit for this
purpose was entrusted by God, through His Church, with
the celebration of the Lord's Supper. Prior to the post-
baptismal celebration of the Lord's Supper, the bishop also
greeted the newly baptized with the words "the Lord be with
thee," to which they responded "And with thy spirit."[18] This
confession was integral, for Hippolytus, to any celebration
of the Lord's Supper. It may be seen that the Spirit was in
like manner bestowed upon presbyters:

But when a presbyter is ordained, the bishop
shall lay his hand upon his head, while the presbyters
touch him, and he shall say according to those things
that were said above, as we have prescribed above
concerning the bishop, praying and saying:

God and Father of our Lord Jesus Christ, look
upon this thy servant, and grant to him the Spirit of

grace and counsel of a presbyter, that he may sustain and govern thy people with a pure heart; as thou didst look upon thy chosen people and didst command Moses that he should choose presbyters, whom thou didst fill with thy Spirit,[19] which thou gavest to thy servant. And now, O Lord, grant that there may be unfailingly preserved amongst us the Spirit of thy grace, and make us worthy that, believing, we may minister to thee in simplicity of heart, praising thee. Through thy Servant Jesus Christ, through whom be to thee glory and honour, with [the] Holy Spirit in the holy church, both now and always and world without end. Amen.[20]

It is thus evident that Hippolytus understood ordination to impart the Holy Spirit to the one being placed into the Office of the Holy Ministry, whether as a bishop or as a presbyter. As such, a presbyter could also be entrusted with the celebration of the Lord's Supper. This giving of the Spirit is made specific to the particular office (". . . grant to him the Spirit of grace and counsel of a presbyter . . ."), and it is also further qualified, as may be seen from the citation immediately following. Nevertheless, the reception of the Spirit for service in the Office of the Holy Ministry is the same in both cases. A striking contrast is found when these are compared with what is said about putting a man into the diaconate:

But the deacon, when he is ordained, is chosen according to those things that were said above, the bishop alone in like manner laying his hands upon him, as we have prescribed. When the deacon is ordained, this is the reason why the bishop alone shall lay his hands upon him: he is not ordained to the priesthood but to serve the bishop and to carry out the bishop's commands. He does not take part in the council of the clergy; he is to attend to his own duties and to make known to the bishop such things as are needful. He does not receive that Spirit that is possessed by the presbytery, in which the presbyters share; he receives only what is confided in him under the bishop's authority.

For this cause the bishop alone shall make a deacon. But on a presbyter, however, the presbyters shall lay their hands because of the common and like Spirit of the clergy. Yet the presbyter has only power to receive; but he has no power to give. For this reason a presbyter does not ordain the clergy; but at the ordination of a presbyter he seals while the bishop ordains.[21]

The ordination prayer does include a petition that God would "grant [the] Holy Spirit of grace and care and diligence to this thy servant, whom thou hast chosen to serve the church . . .",[22] but distinctions are clearly made between the spiritual blessings given to a deacon and the Spirit which is bestowed upon the clergy proper, that is, upon the bishops and presbyters. While a presbyter was here not permitted to ordain, no such restrictions were placed upon the celebration of the Lord's Supper. This further suggests that presbyters were also entrusted with the celebration of the Lord's Supper, although perhaps only in the absence of a bishop. Laymen are specifically forbidden to "celebrate" (i.e., to bless the bread) at a "blessing" meal.[23] It is explicitly stated in the context that this is not a Lord's Supper, and suggests that with such meals, in the absence of a bishop, the blessing of either a deacon or a presbyter will suffice.[24] Nevertheless, when it is observed that a layman is forbidden to bless the bread at a blessing meal, it is scarcely imaginable that he would be permitted to celebrate the Lord's Supper. Rather, the celebration of the Lord's Supper was reliable where one was certain that the Spirit was present. One could be confident that the Spirit would descend upon that celebration of the Lord's Supper which was celebrated by one to whom the Spirit had been given for that purpose; that is, one who had been entrusted with placing the Lord's words upon the elements. It has been seen that such a one was a bishop or a presbyter, not a deacon or a layman. The relation between the Office of the Holy Ministry and the celebration of the Lord's Supper, according to the *Apostolic Tradition*, was exclusive. Apart from the office, and the Spirit who accompanies it, there is no authority to forgive sins, and thus there can be no celebration of the Lord's Supper.

One further observation based upon what has been seen in the *Apostolic Tradition* is in order. When a holder of the Office of the Holy Ministry celebrates the Lord's Supper today, he begins by saying "The Lord be with you," and his congregation responds, "and with your spirit."[25] This response has continued to be part of the service in liturgical churches to this very day. Whether intentionally or in ignorance, whenever a congregation has spoken the words "and with your spirit" to the celebrant at the Lord's Supper, they have confessed that the holders of the Office of the Holy Ministry, particularly the one standing before them, are alone entrusted by the Lord with the celebration of His Supper.[26]

94

Notes:

[1] Concerning the importance of the title, see Chapter IV. The title amounts to a declaration that the author is preserving the apostolic faith against novelties, which cannot be apostolic, and therefore cannot be from the Lord.

[2] John E. Stam, Episcopacy in the Apostolic Tradition of Hippolytus (Basel: Friedrich Reinhardt Kommissionsverlag, 1969), pp. 8-9.

[3] Hippolyte de Rome, La Tradition Apostolique, Sources Chrétiennes vol. 11, 2nd ed., Bernard Botte, ed. (Paris: Les Éditions du Cerf, 1984), p. 37. (Hereafter "Sources.")

[4] R. C. D. Jasper and G. J. Cuming, Prayers of the Eucharist: Early and Reformed, 3rd rev. ed. (New York: Pueblo Publishing Co., 1987), p. 31.

[5] Joseph A. Jungmann, The Mass of the Roman Rite: Its Origins and Development, vol. I, trans. Francis A. Brunner (New York: Benziger Brothers, 1951), p. 28.

[6] Ibid., p. 32.

[7] Paul F. Bradshaw, Ordination Rites of the Ancient Churches (New York: Pueblo Publishing Company, 1990), pp. 3-4. Stählin argues that Hippolytus' work may be seen as more generally representative of the state of liturgics at the beginning of the third century: "Die entgegengesetzte Auffassung, das Werk Hippolyts stelle eine private Arbeit des schismatischen Bischofs dar, . . . hat sich nicht durchsetzen können. Schon die außerordentlich starke wirkung, die die Kirchenordnung im Osten gehabt hat (es sind syrische, koptische, äthiopische und arabische Übersetzungen erhalten), spricht dagegen. Freilich zeigt die Apostolische Überlieferung deutlich das persönliche Gepräge ihres Verfassers. Der Wortlaut wird wohl auf ihn zurück gehen. Dei Struktur ist aber im wesent-lichen die der Tradition." Rudolph Stählin, "Die Geschichte des christlichen Gottesdienstes von der Urkirche bis zur Gaegenwart," in Karl Ferdinand Müller and Walter Blankenburg, eds., Leiturgia, vol. 1 (Kassel: Johannes Stauda Verlag, 1954), p. 20, n. 54.

[8] Bernard Botte has provided an edition of the Latin text, as well as the Greek text of the ordination rite. For the sections which are pertinent to this study, the reader is referred to appendices 1 and 2.

[9] Hippolytus, Apostolic Tradition I.1. This paragraph is translated from the Latin. Burton Scott Easton, ed. and trans., The Apostolic Tradition of Hippolytus (Cambridge University Press, 1934), p. 33. For the Latin text, see Sources 11:38, 40.

[10] Jasper and Cuming, p. 31.

[11] See in this regard Hippolytus' description of the Montanists in his work, Refutation of All Heresies, VIII.19. He writes:

"But there are others who themselves are even more heretical [αιρετικ-ωτεροι] in nature (than the foregoing), and are Phrygians by birth. These have been rendered victims of error from being previously captivated by (two) wretched women, called a certain Priscilla and Maximilla, whom they supposed to be prophetesses. And they asserted that into these the Paraclete Spirit had departed; and antecedently to them, they in like manner consider Montanus as a prophet ... And they allege that they have learned something more [πλειον] through these, than from law, and prophets, and the Gospels. But they magnify these wretched women above the Apostles and every gift of Grace, so that some of them presume to assert that there is in them something superior [πλειον, i.e."something more than," as above] to Christ. These acknowledge God to be the Father of the universe, and Creator of all things, similarly with the Church, and (receive) many things as the Gospel testifies concerning Christ. *They introduce, however, the novelties* [καινιζουσι] *of fasts, and feasts, and meals of parched food, and repasts of radishes, alleging that they have been instructed by women.*" (Italics added). Translation in Alexander Roberts and James Donaldson, eds., The Ante-Nicene Fathers, 10 vols. (Grand Rapids, MI: Wm. B. Eerdmans Publishing Company, 1986), vol. 5, p. 123. (Hereafter ANF). This paragraph is listed as no. 12 instead of no. 19 in this translation. For the Greek text, see: Hippolytus, Refutatio Omnium Haeresium, edited by Miroslav Marcovich (Berlin: Walter de Gruyter, 1986), p. 338.

[12] For a description of Hippolytus' disagreements with Callistus, see Easton, pp. 18-24.

[13] This parenthetical is not found in the Greek *Epitome,* but is included in the Latin, Ethiopic, the *Apostolic Constitutions,* and other corroborating sources.

[14] John 20:22-23.

[15] Hippolytus, *Apostolic Tradition* I.2, 3. Trans. by Easton, pp. 33-35. The Latin text of these two sections, and the Greek text of the prayer (section 3) have been reproduced at the end of this book in Appendices 1 and 2, respectively, from the texts provided in Sources 11:40, 42, 44, 46, 48. Lietzmann provides a most helpful comment concerning the sacrificial language which one finds connected with the Lord's Supper in Hippolytus:

"It is from this obvious point of view that we have to understand likewise the *form* of the sacrifice in the Hippolytan liturgy of the Supper: the whole thing becomes coherent and easily comprehensible without resorting to artificial explanations. One sacrifices something to God by laying it upon the table or raising it heavenward and saying a prayer over it. This applies to bread and wine, just as much as to oil and olives, milk and cheese, fruits of the field and other gifts. The idea of sacrificing to God gifts in kind is blended with the ancient spiritual conception that prayer is the only worthy Christian sacrifice." Thus Hans Lietzmann, Mass and the Lord's Supper, trans. Dorothea H. G. Reeve (Leiden: E. J. Brill, 1979), p. 151. Understood in this way, Hippolytus is a far cry from the "unbloody sacrifice" of the *Apostolic Constitutions* of a century and a half later.

[16] Hippolytus, *Apostolic Tradition* I.4. Trans. by Easton, p. 35. The Latin text of I.4, up to the point of the English translation provided here, may

be found at the end of this volume in appendix 1.

[17] See Noële Maurice Denis-Boulet and Roger Béraudy, <u>The Church at Prayer</u>, vol. 2, *The Eucharist*, A. G. Martimort, ed., trans. Daniel Farrelly (New York: Herder and Herder, 1973), pages 83-84: "In the Bible, for example in the Book of Judges when the angel says to Gideon, 'Yahweh be with you' (6:12) and in many similar passages, this is a statement and not a wish or a greeting (except in Ruth 2:4, where the master addresses the phrase to the harvesters). In Luke 1:28 the formula follows the words 'Hail, full of grace.' This was evidently far from customary, for Mary 'asked herself what manner of greeting this might be'. But throughout the Scriptures there is mention of an active presence of God in man (the very meaning of the word *Emmanuel*: Mt 1:23), in harmony with the dynamism of the Spirit which has been given to him (see especially Ac 10:38 and Jn 3:2). Thus the liturgical greeting *Dominus vobiscum*, and its reply, equally well vouched for, *Et cum spiritu tuo* . . . — is deeply rooted in the revelation of the Old and New Testaments: God is present in the assembly. The celebrant, for his part, being called to pray in the name of all, has special need of the active presence of the Holy Spirit."

[18] Ibid., II.21. Trans. by Easton (and cited as II.22), p. 48. For the Latin, see <u>Sources</u> 11:90.

[19] Numbers 11:24-25. Again, and now in the liturgy, the church confesses the continuity of the Office of the Holy Ministry in the Old Testament with the Office of the Holy Ministry in the New Testament. In both cases, the guarantor of the Office is the Holy Spirit.

[20] Hippolytus, *Apostolic Tradition* I.7. Trans. (cited as I.8) by Easton, p. 37. For the Latin, see <u>Sources</u> 11:56, 58.

[21] Ibid., I.8. Trans. (cited as I.9) by Easton, p. 38. For the Latin, see <u>Sources</u> 11:58, 60.

[22] Ibid., I.8. Trans. (cited as I.9) by Easton, pp. 38-39. For the Latin, see <u>Sources</u> 11:62.

[23] Ibid., III.28. The English translation (cited as III.26) reads: "But if [only] laymen meet, let them not act presumptuously, for a layman cannot bless the blessed bread." Easton, p. 51. The Latin reads: "*Si laici fuerint in unum, cum moderatione agant. Laicus enim benedictionem facere non potest.*" <u>Sources</u> 11:108.

[24] Ibid., III.26. The English translation (cited as the first part of III.26) reads: "This service . . . is 'a Blessing,' not 'a Thanksgiving,' as is . . . the Body of the Lord." Easton, p. 50. The Latin reads: ". . . *quia eulogia est et non eucharistia sicut caro domini.*" <u>Sources</u> 11:102.

[25] The three orders of the divine service in the <u>Lutheran Book of Worship</u> (Minneapolis, MN: Augsburg Publishing House, 1978), have substituted the words "and also with you" for the response, "and with your spirit" (pp. 68, 88, 109), which change is without precedent in either the Lutheran liturgical heritage specifically, or the ancient liturgical heritage of the Church

catholic. The use of this novelty effectively omits the confession of the Office of the Holy Ministry which has been included in the liturgies of the Church for over one and a half millennia, and replaces it with a meaningless banality. When the confession of the Office of the Holy Ministry is omitted, the confession of the relation of that office to the celebration of the Lord's Supper is omitted with it. This same innovation has been incorporated into Divine Service II of <u>Lutheran Worship</u> (St. Louis, MO: Concordia Publishing House, 1982), pp. 170, 189. To the credit of the latter, it does continue to provide the option of having what was always in the liturgy, i.e. the response "and with your spirit," which is the Church's liturgical confession of the Office of the Holy Ministry. This is found in Divine Service I, pp. 144-145. One principle that was clearly important to Hippolytus in his liturgical formulæ was the fact that that which is new and innovative cannot possibly be at the same time apostolic. That which has been handed down from the Lord through His apostles cannot have been concocted yesterday. This is a principle to which American Lutheranism would do well to recall itself.

[26] Concerning the prayer of consecration spoken over the elements, Easton comments: "The liturgical influence of this prayer has been incalculable. It is the basis of the liturgy in the Constitutions, through which it determined the form and in part the wording of the great Eastern liturgies, St James, St Basil and St Chrysostom. In the other Eastern rites its influence is usually perceptible, though less fundamental, while in the Ethiopic church it is still used almost unchanged." Easton, pp. 73-74. One can hardly say less of other aspects of Hippolytus' church order. The words of the communion preface are employed almost universally in liturgical churches.

CHAPTER IX

THE APOSTOLIC CONSTITUTIONS
(Διαταγαι των Αγιων Αποστολων)

The *Apostolic Constitutions* appear to have originated around A.D. 375, and were quite probably the work of an Arian compiler.[1] The Arian leanings of the compiler are important to certain doctrinal aspects of the contents of the work. R. C. D. Jasper and G. J. Cuming go so far as to at least imply the possibility that the compiler was Julian, an Eunomian bishop in Cilicia around A.D. 364.[2]

The *Apostolic Constitutions*, particularly the liturgy contained in the eighth book thereof, belongs to the West Syrian (Antiochene) liturgical family.[3] The Liturgy of St. James (which is discussed in Chapter XI) also belongs to this liturgical family, and its liturgical formulation was apparently influenced by this liturgy. Louis Bouyer rejects the notion that the liturgy contained in the *Apostolic Constitutions* is "a liturgy-on-paper which could never have been used as it stands on account of its prolixity," and argues that it was used in Antioch in the fourth century.[4]

The compilation does nothing, however, to change the view held by the documents upon which it is based concerning the relation of the Office of the Holy Ministry to the celebration of the Lord's Supper. One example of this may be found in the following:

> By thy bishop, O man, God adopts thee for His child . . .

For if the divine oracle says, concerning our parents according to the flesh, "Honour thy father and thy mother . . ." how much more should the word exhort you to honour your spiritual parents, and to love them as your benefactors and ambassadors with God, who have regenerated you by water, and endued you with the fulness of the Holy Spirit, who have fed you with the word as with milk, who have nourished you with doctrine, who have confirmed you by their admonitions, who have imparted to you the saving body and precious blood of Christ, who have loosed you from your sins, who have made you partakers of the holy and sacred eucharist, who have admitted you to be partakers and fellow-heirs of the promise of God![5]

This passage has as its basis the text of the *Didascalia* 9:33. It does not introduce anything new in a doctrinal sense. Its inclusion in the *Apostolic Constitutions* serves to preserve the same connection between the sin-forgiving office (i.e., bishop) and the celebration of the Lord's Supper. The *Apostolic Constitutions* here continue to recognize that the bishop is entrusted with stewardship of all of the means of sin-forgiving grace, and the Lord's Supper in particular. Another passage pertinent to this study is cited by the *Apostolic Constitutions* from the same source, this time with a noteworthy editorial alteration:

And if a presbyter comes from another parish, let him be received to communion by the presbyters; if a deacon, by the deacons; if a bishop, let him sit with the bishop, and be allowed the same honour with himself; and thou, O bishop, shalt desire him to speak to the people words of instruction: for the exhortation and admonition of strangers is very acceptable, and exceeding profitable. For, as the Scripture says, "no prophet is accepted in his own country." Thou shalt also permit him to offer the Eucharist; but if, out of reverence to thee, and as a wise man, to preserve the honour belonging to thee, he will not offer, at least thou shalt compel him to give the blessing to the people.[6]

This admonition is taken nearly verbatim from the *Didascalia*. The most striking difference is that, in the *Didascalia*, if the visiting bishop declined to be the primary celebrant at the Lord's Supper, he was still to be encouraged to say the words which were spoken over the cup. By the time the *Apostolic Constitutions* were compiled, the practice of permitting a joint celebration of the Lord's Supper by two bishops was no longer in use, so that the visiting bishop was instead given the honor of giving the blessing.[7]

It has been observed above that part of the *Apostolic Constitutions* appears to be based upon the *Didache*. As such, the similarities and differences are noteworthy. Chapter seven of the *Didache* gives instructions concerning Baptism: "In regard to Baptism—baptize thus: . . ."[8] Critical here is that the identity of the addressee is never specifically stated. In his revision in the corresponding chapter of the seventh book of the *Apostolic Constitutions*, the compiler opted for greater specificity: "Now concerning baptism, O bishop, or presbyter, we have already given direction, and we now say, that thou shalt so baptize as the Lord commanded us . . ."[9] The *Apostolic Constitutions* identify the addressee as either a bishop or a presbyter. The prayer of the *Didache* 9:1-5 is expanded, most notably by the inclusion of the following:

We also, our Father, thank Thee for the precious blood

of Jesus Christ, which was shed for us, and for His precious body, whereof we celebrate this representation [αντιτυπα], as Himself [sic] appointed us, "to show forth His death."[10]

While it has been argued that chapter nine of the *Didache* may well have been a prayer spoken over an *agape* meal, it is apparent that the compiler of the *Apostolic Constitutions* understood it to pertain to the celebration of the Lord's Supper, and modified the prayer accordingly. Even the compiler's modifications, however, do not connect this prayer with a celebrant of any sort, let alone one who holds the Office of the Holy Ministry. To find such a connection, one turns to the compiler's incorporation of the *Apostolic Tradition* of Hippolytus. Joseph A. Jungmann comments upon this:

> The eighth book of the *Apostolic Constitutions* is, in its structure and legal regulations, little more in general than a revision of the *Apostolic Tradition* of Hippolytus. But as regards the Mass-liturgy the traces of Hippolytus' draft are faint. In its place we have the usage, by now somewhat fixed, of the Syrian capital.[11]

The ordination prayer found in book eight of the *Apostolic Constitutions* is based upon the episcopal ordination prayer of Hippolytus, but it has been expanded, and several differences are noteworthy. Although the importance of the power of the Holy Spirit is by no means decreased, the admonition to silent prayer prior to the ordination no longer includes an admonition to pray for the descent of the Spirit. Of the presbyters and bishops there present, three of the senior bishops gather at the altar, and one of them offers the lengthy ordination prayer. It includes a detailed enumeration of many of those who had served God as priests in times past, beginning with Abel and Seth(!), and continuing on with Abraham, Moses, Aaron, and so forth. Several parts of the ordaining bishop's prayer call for quotation:

> Do Thou, by us, pour down the influence [δυναμιν, "power"] of Thy free Spirit, through the mediation of Thy Christ ... Grant by Thy name, ... that this Thy servant, whom thou hast chosen to be a bishop, may feed Thy holy flock, and discharge the office of an high priest to Thee, ... Grant to him, O Lord Almighty, through thy Christ, the fellowship [μετουσιαψ] of the Holy Spirit, that he may have power to remit sins according to Thy command;[12] ... to offer to Thee a pure and unbloody sacrifice [αν αι μακτον θυσιαν], which by Thy Christ Thou hast appointed as the mystery of the new covenant ...[13]

This reproduces Hippolytus' prayer that God would "pour forth now that power, which is thine, of thy royal Spirit." Arian theological considerations, which did not recognize the Holy Spirit as a distinct person of the Triune God, may have resulted in the elimination of the silent prayer for the descent of the Spirit before the service of ordination, but this is speculation. The application of the words of John 20:21-23 to what happens at ordination remains unchanged. Neither was there a change in what the congregation said in response to the newly ordained at the completion of his ordination:

> And after the prayer let one of the bishops elevate the sacrifice upon the hands of him that is ordained, ... let him that is ordained salute the Church, say-

> ing, The grace of our Lord Jesus Christ, the love of God and the Father, and the fellowship of the Holy Ghost, be with you all; and let them all answer, And with Thy Spirit.[14]

Once again, the congregation acknowledges the ordinand's reception of the Office of the Holy Ministry by speaking of his "Spirit"; that is, he was understood to be the recipient of a unique bestowal of a gift of the Holy Spirit, along with which came the authority to remit sins, and thus to celebrate the Lord's Supper. At the conclusion of the ordination there follows the divine service, made up mostly of lengthy prayers offered by the bishop. Then, after all of the "catechumens, . . . hearers, . . . unbelievers, [and] . . . heterodox"[15] have been dismissed, the communion liturgy begins.

> Let the high priest, therefore, together with the priests, pray by himself; and let him put on his shining garment, and stand at the altar, and make the sign of the cross upon his forehead with his hand, and say: The grace of Almighty God, and the love of our Lord Jesus Christ, and the fellowship of the Holy Ghost, be with you all.   And let all with one voice say: And with thy spirit.
> The high priest: Lift up your mind.
> All the people: We lift it up unto the Lord.
> The high priest: Let us give thanks to the Lord.
> All the people: It is meet and right so to do.
> Then let the high priest say: It is very meet and right before all things to sing an hymn to Thee, who art the true God . . .[16]

Any novel doctrines having been introduced by the Arians notwithstanding, no one dared to tamper with the responsive communion preface part of the liturgical confession. As this lengthy prayer of consecration continues, the consecrating words which Christ used when He instituted His Supper are included:

> Being mindful, therefore, of those things that He endured for our sakes, we give Thee thanks, O God Almighty, not in such a manner as we ought, but as we are able, and fulfil His constitution: "For in the same night that He was betrayed, He took bread" in His holy and undefiled hands, and, looking up to Thee His God and Father, "He brake it, and gave it to His disciples, saying, This is the mystery [μυστηριον] of the new covenant: take of it, and eat. This is my body, which is broken for many, for the remission of sins." In like manner also "He took the cup," and mixed it of wine and water, and sanctified it, and delivered it to them saying: "Drink ye all of this; for this is my blood which is shed for many, for the remission of sins: do this in remembrance of me. For as often as ye eat this bread and drink this cup, ye do show forth my death until I come."[17]

We saw that the term μυστηριον was not used as a technical designation for the sacraments until the third or fourth century. It is apparently used in precisely that way here, and one may therefore assume that the compiler understood 1 Cor. 4:1 to indicate that stewardship of the Lord's Supper was entrusted to holders of the Office of the Holy Ministry. Whether such an interpretation of this particular text of Scripture is at work here or not, the compiler does not in any way modify Hippolytus' exclusive connection of the Office and the celebration of the Lord's Supper. What is new to the prayer in the *Apostolic Constitutions* is the introduction of an *Epiklesis* into the prayer of consecration:

> And do Thou accept them, to the honour of Thy Christ, and send down upon this sacrifice Thine Holy Spirit, the Witness of the Lord Jesus' sufferings, that he may show [αποφηψη] this bread to be the body of Thy Christ, and the cup to be the blood of Thy Christ, ...[18]

The effect of such a prayer is to suggest that the dominical words, spoken by one to whom the Spirit has been given, do not yet suffice for the Spirit to come upon the elements and cause them to be the body and blood of Christ; a special prayer for the sending down of the Holy Spirit is also prayed. In any case, it is clear that the one who is to pray that prayer is one who holds the Office of the Holy Ministry.

    In conclusion, it may be said that the *Apostolic Constitutions* are more a compilation of the other three documents than they are a serious modification of them. Perhaps the most startlingly novel introduction is the notion of the Lord's Supper as an "unbloody sacrifice" of Christ. Previous church orders, when referring to a "sacrifice," appear to speak of the offerings of the people, particularly the offering of bread and wine which are then used in the Lord's Supper, but the notion and particularly the wording of "unbloody sacrifice" seem to be new. While this is a novelty, and it appears in an Arian document, one may not conclude on that basis that this is necessarily an Arian novelty.

    Arian doctrine apparently slips in at several points, but part of the subtle nature of the heresy was that its proponents proved quite adept at reinterpreting doctrinal and liturgical formulations in a way that rendered orthodox terminology compatible with an Arian doctrinal position.

Most of the modifications seem rather to accommodate historical changes in the practices of "Christian" (be they orthodox or Arian) churches, such as the discontinuation of *agape* meals or con-celebrations of the Lord's Supper. The exclusive relation of the Office of the Holy Ministry to the celebration of the Lord's Supper is never modified in the slightest.

The *Apostolic Constitutions* had a particularly strong influence upon the further development of the West Syrian (also known as "Antiochene" or "Jacobite") liturgical family. It also had some influence on the Coptic (otherwise known as "Alexandrian" or "Markan") liturgical family.[19] One liturgy from each of these families will be further discussed below.

Notes:

[1] Arthur Vööbus, The Didascalia Apostolorum in Syriac, vol. 1, tome 176 (Louvain: Corpus Scriptorum Christianorum Orientalum, 1979), pp. 30-31. According to Metzger, F. X. Funk attempted to preserve the *Apostolic Constitutions* from the charge of Arianism in his *Didascalia et Constitutiones Apostolorum* 1, but this attempt has been broadly refuted in scholarly circles. Marcel Metzger, "The Didascalia and the Constitutiones Apostolorum," in The Eucharist of the Early Christians, trans. Matthew J. O'Connell (New York: Pueblo Publishing Company, 1978), pp. 196-197, 214. See on this point F. X. Funk, ed., Didascalia et Constitutiones Apostolorum (Torino: Bogetta d'Erasmo, 1959), p. xv.

[2] R. C. D. Jasper and G. J. Cuming, Prayers of the Eucharist, Early and reformed (New York: Pueblo Publishing Company, 1980), p. 100.

[3] Louis Bouyer, Eucharist, trans. Charles Underhill Quinn (Notre Dame, IN: University of Notre Dame Press, 1968), p. 244.

[4] Ibid., pp. 250-251.

[5] *Constitutions of the Holy Apostles*, Book II, 5:32-33, in ANF, vol. 7, p. 412. For the Greek, see Les Constitutions Apostoliques, vol. I, Marcel Metzger, ed., Sources 320:252, 254.

[6] *Constitutions of the Holy Apostles*, Book II, 7:58, in Roberts, ANF, vol. 7, p. 422.

108

[7] Metzger, in The Eucharist of the Early Christians, p. 202.

[8] *Didache* 7:1, as cited in William A. Jurgens, The Faith of the Early Fathers, vol. 1 (Collegeville, MN: The Liturgical Press, 1970), p. 2. The Greek reads: Περι δε του βαπτισματος, ουθωτω βαπτισατε. J. B. Lightfoot and J. R. Harmer, eds., The Apostolic Fathers (Grand Rapids, MI: Baker Book House, 1988), p. 221.

[9] *Constitutions of the Holy Apostles*, Book VII, 2:22, in Roberts, ANF, vol. 7, p. 469. The Greek reads: "Περι δε βαπτι σματος, ω επισκοπε η πρεσβυωτερε, ηδη μεν και προτερον διεταζαμεθα, και νυν δε φαμεν οτι ουτως βαπτισεις ως ο Κυριος ημιν δι εταζατο λεγων." *Les Constitutions Apostoliques*, vol. III, Marcel Metzger, ed., Sources (1987), 336:46.

[10] Ibid., Book VII, 2:25, in Roberts, ANF, vol. 7, p. 470. The Greek reads: "Ετι ευξαριστουμεν, Πατερ ημων, υπερ του τιμιου αιματος Ιησου Χριστου του εκχυθεντος υπερ ημων και του τιμιου σωματος, ου και αντιτυπα ταυτα επι τελουμεν, αυτου διαταξαμενου ημιν καταγγελλειν τον αυτου θανατον: δι αυτου γαρ σοι και η δοξα εις τους αιωνας: αμην." Metzger, Sources 336:54.

[11] Joseph A. Jungmann, The Mass of the Roman Rite: Its Origins and Development, vol. I, trans. Francis A. Brunner (New York: Benziger Brothers, 1951), p. 35.

[12] See Chapter I, John 20:22-23.

[13] *Constitutions of the Holy Apostles*, Book VIII, 5:5-7, cited as VIII, 2:5 in Roberts, ANF, vol. 7, pp. 482-483. For the Greek, see Metzger, Sources 336:146, 148.

[14] Ibid., Book VIII, 2:5, in Roberts, ANF, vol. 7, p. 483. For the Greek, see Metzger, Sources 336:150.

[15] "... the deacon shall immediately say, Let none of the catechumens, let none of the hearers, let none of the unbelievers, let none of the heterodox, stay here." *Constitutions of the Holy Apostles*, Book VIII, 2:12, in Roberts, ANF, vol. 7, p. 486. For the Greek, see Metzger, Sources 336:176.

[16] *Constitutions of the Holy Apostles*, Book VIII, 2:12, in Roberts, ANF, vol. 7, p. 486. The Greek, beginning with "The grace of Almighty God," and ending with "It is meet and right so to do," reads:

Η χαρις του παντοκρατορος Θεου και η αγαπη του Κυριου ημων Ιησου Χριστου και η κοινωνια Πνευματος εστω μετα παντων υμων.

Και παντες συμφωνω λεγετωσαν, οτι:

Και μετα του πνευματος σου.

Και ο αρχιερευς: Ανω τον νουν.

Και παντες: Εχομεν προς τον Κυριον.

Και ο αρχιερευς: Ευξαριστησωμεν τω Κυριω.

Και παντες: Αξιον και δικαιον.

Metzger, Sources 336:178, 180.

[17] Ibid., Roberts, ANF, vol. 7, p. 489. The Greek may be found in Metzger,

Sources 336:196, 198.

[18] Ibid., in Roberts, ANF, vol. 7, p. 489. For the Greek, see Metzger, Sources 336:198, 200. This translation may be compared with the one found in Jasper and Cuming, pp. 110-111.

[19] Paul F. Bradshaw, Ordination Rites of the Ancient Churches (New York: Pueblo Publishing Company, 1990), p. 4.

PART III:

THE TESTIMONY OF SELECTED PRIMARY
LITURGIES

CHAPTER X

THE LITURGY OF SAINTS ADDAI AND MARI

Lucien Deiss divides the Eastern liturgies into two groups, the Alexandrian and the Antiochene. The Antiochene liturgies are further divided into West Syrian and East Syrian types. The liturgy of *Addai and Mari* belongs to the East Syrian type and apparently dates to the third century.[1] Edward C. Ratcliff in particular attempts to reconstruct the original form of the liturgy by "reconstructing the anaphora of Addai and Mari as it was about A.D. 500," and finds in it the older, parent form also of the anaphoras of Nestorius and of Theodore "the Interpreter" (Mopsuestia).[2] Kenneth Stevenson notes, "Addai and Mari may yet be more primitive than Hippolytus."[3] Charles E. Hammond considers this liturgy to be the norm for the East Syrian Family of liturgies.[4] Joseph A. Jungmann comments further upon this liturgical family:

> The liturgy of the primitive Church in Palestine was certainly not Greek but Aramaic. Aramaic—that is, Syriac—was, by force of necessity, also the language of the ecclesiastical liturgy which penetrated to the North and East beyond the bounds of the Roman Empire. The liturgy that thus evolved was the *East-Syrian*.
>
> The East-Syrian liturgy is known also as the *Nestorian*, because of the desertion to Nestorius, or as *Chaldean*,

with reference to the groups who returned to communion with Rome. It is still employed by the descendants of these Christian peoples: by the Syrians in Mesopotamia and by the Christians living on the Malabar coast (the most important mission territory of the East-Syrians). The East-Syrian Mass, as recorded in the oldest documents, gives indications of a period of Greek influence, but this soon came to an end as this part of Christendom became gradually isolated.[5]

Paul F. Bradshaw comments upon the extent of the isolation, liturgical and otherwise, of this tradition:

> Although originally part of the Antiochene patriarchate, Christians in East Syria not only had a strongly Semitic background, but also spoke Syriac rather than Greek and lived under Persian rather than Roman rule. Because of these factors, they largely escaped Antiochene liturgical influence and developed quite distinct practices of their own. After their rejection of the Council of Ephesus in A.D. 431, they followed the Nestorian tradition and were thus effectively isolated from the rest of Christendom as the Assyrian Church of the East.[6]

The East Syrian liturgical tradition thus appears to have originated quite early (thus Stevenson), and is the result of an almost completely independent development.[7] The liturgy of *Addai and Mari* is most valuable in this regard, as a strong basis for confidence has been provided that later or alien doctrinal viewpoints have not been imposed on it, and that what is here analyzed is indeed a clear liturgical confession of the faith of the East Syrian Christians.

Perhaps the most startling feature of this liturgy is that the words of institution are nowhere to be found. The question may be asked: Without the *verba* being included in the liturgy, can this be understood to be a celebration of the Lord's Supper? For this, one turns to the text of the liturgy itself.

> At the conclusion of the litany, the priest prays the prayer of the Inclination. Following this, the deacon says:
> Let him that hath not received baptism depart.
> Let him that doth not receive the sign of life depart.
> Let him that doth not accept it depart.
> Go, ye hearers, and watch the doors.[8]

It is difficult to imagine that such care would have been taken to protect that which was not the Lord's Supper. The Offertory and the Creed follow. Prior to the salutation, "Peace be with you," the priest offers the following prayer. The text specifies that it is offered by the priest.

> Priest: We will give you thanks, Lord, for the abundant riches of your grace toward us. For when we were weak sinners, you made us worthy, in keeping with your great mercy, of celebrating the holy mysteries of the body and blood of your Christ. We implore your help. Strengthen our souls, that we may celebrate with perfect charity and sincere love the gift you have given us. We praise you, we glorify you, we give you thanks, we adore you now . . .
>
> People: Amen.
> Priest: Peace be with you.

People: With you and with your spirit.[9]

At this point, when the priest has spoken the peace to the people, the preface continues. This is followed by the *Sanctus*, and then by the Intercessory Prayers. The conclusion of the part of the prayer offered by the priest prior to the *Epiklesis* reads as follows:

> (Priest):   And we too, Lord, your weak, frail, and lowly servants, who have gathered and are standing before you at this moment, we have received from tradition the rite that has its origin in you. We rejoice and give glory, we exalt and commemorate, we praise and celebrate this great and awesome mystery of the passion, the death, and the resurrection of our Lord Jesus Christ.[10]

Immediately the *Epiklesis* follows:

Deacon: Be silent . . .

Priest: May your Holy Spirit come, Lord, may he rest upon this offering of your servants, may he bless and sanctify it, so that it may win[11] for us, Lord, the forgiveness of offenses and the remission of sins, the great hope of the resurrection of the dead, and new life in the kingdom of heaven with all those who have been pleasing to you.[12]

Finally, there is the Doxology:

[Priest:]   Because of your all-embracing, wonderful plan which you have carried out in our regard, we give you thanks and glorify you ceaselessly in your Church which you have redeemed through the precious blood of your Christ. With open mouths and faces unveiled we present you with . . .

People: Amen.[13]

The absence of the words of institution may now be addressed. This is a most important point, as it may cast doubt upon whether or not this is, in fact, a Lord's Supper. One may only investigate the relation between the Office of the Holy Ministry and the celebration of the Lord's Supper in this liturgy when it has been established that the Lord's Supper is indeed being celebrated.

One response of western liturgical analysts is to suggest that *Addai and Mari* is not truly a celebration of the Lord's Supper. One of those to argue in this vein is Edward C. Ratcliff. After claiming that the *Sanctus* is the result of an intrusion and that the position of the *Epiklesis* suggests Greek influence, he offers the following:

This is a ευχαριστια pure and simple. There is in it no thought of oblation, whether of bread and wine or of the Body and Blood of Christ made present by consecration. But it is a ευχαριστια of a particular kind. It is commemorative of Christ's death and resurrection; and the commemoration is one, not in word only, but also in act, in an imitating of Christ's act, for the ευχαριστια is said over bread and wine (at one time, perhaps over bread alone), and the bread and wine thus blessed are eaten and drunk by the assemblage. The communal character of the rite is marked; it is the act of all present, and all are to answer Amen at the end of the prayer.

The rite has no necessary connexion with the Last Supper; the connexion is rather with the Emmaus Supper. But while it is not the Mass, so also the rite is not merely an Agape. It is quite definitely a οραμα, something ceremonially done. It comes somewhere between the Mass and Agape, and it has affinity in a general kind of way with the *intention* of the ευχαριστια μετα το εμπλησθηναι in Cap. X of the Didache.[14] It may be said that the anaphora of Addai and Mari preserves to us a relic of a form of the Eucharist, which, once more general at least in the East, eventually gave way to the Last Supper form of the rite.[15]

This line of argument presupposes two different "eucharistic traditions," much as does Hans Lietzmann. It is not surprising that Richardson (of the "further inquiry" appended to the English translation of Lietzmann's work) is quite sympathetic with Ratcliff's understanding of *Addai and Mari* as a "primitive eucharistia."[16]

There seem to be some weaknesses in Ratcliff's suggestions. Perhaps central to his comments is the suggestion that *Addai and Mari* is to be connected not with the Last Supper but with the Emmaus meal. The evidence simply does not bear this out. The prayer prior to the communion refers to the "celebrating the holy mysteries of the body and blood of your Christ." There is the confession, "we have received from tradition the rite that has its origin in you." If this refers back to 1 Cor. 11:2, it would probably refer to the Lord's Supper, about which Paul speaks later in the same chapter. If it refers to the apostle's απο του κυριου immediately preceding his recounting of the words of institution (1 Cor. 11:23), the connection would be even closer. The confession, "we . . . commemorate this great and awesome mystery of the passion, the death, and the resurrection of our Lord Jesus Christ," apparently refers to Paul's words in 1 Cor. 11:26. The text of the *Epiklesis* specifically prays that what is being celebrated would be for "the forgiveness of offenses and the remission of sins," which would confess the words of the Lord in Matt. 26:28, and which has no evident connection with what happened at Emmaus. In short, the conclusion that *Addai and Mari* intends to be a celebration of the Lord's Supper is inescapable.

Louis Bouyer takes a very different approach. Apparently presupposing that it is probable neither that the Lord's Supper is absent from *Addai and Mari* nor that the Lord's words would not be spoken at a celebration of the Lord's Supper, Bouyer simply inserts them immediately prior to the *Epiklesis*. This is not to suggest that his suggestion is capricious. Citing Theodore of Mopsuestia, he presents a respectable case that the words of institution *might* have originally been included.[17] That they *were* originally included, however, simply cannot be demonstrated.[18]

The present author believes a third approach to this issue seems to be in order. The Lord's Supper is the Lord's Supper because the words of the Lord are put upon the bread and wine. It may have been believed, however, that it was not absolutely necessary that those words be *repeated* for them to be *applied* to the bread and wine. The liturgical confession of *Addai and Mari* very clearly applies the words of Christ to the bread and wine. This approach apparently underlies the analysis of Bryan Spinks:

> The words 'received by tradition the example (model) which is from you' are clearly a reference to the institution of the eucharist, and one might speculate as to

whether there is some connection here with 1 Cor. 11.23, where, underlying Paul's Greek, the Rabbinical technical terms *qibbel*, received, and *masar*, delivered, are used to introduce the institution. Perhaps we have here an East Syrian 'shorthand' narrative of institution.[19]

Thus, *Addai and Mari* may be acknowledged as genuinely that which the Lord instituted, "the eucharist," that is, the Lord's Supper.[20] One might even suggest that it is a very pointed confession that it is the words spoken by the Lord (once for all) at the Last Supper which cause the elements to be the body and blood of Christ, and not the repetition of those words by the one who holds the Office of the Holy Ministry. Finally, even if one were still to insist that this is not a true Lord's Supper, it is quite apparent that the East Syrians understood it to be one, and therefore that which is said to and done by the office-holder would still be a reflection of what the East Syrian Church understood to be the relation of the Office of the Holy Ministry to the celebration of the Lord's Supper.

Having established that *Addai and Mari* was, at the very least, intended to be a liturgy of the Lord's Supper, one may proceed with an analysis of the text. It has been seen that the text begins with a prayer of thanksgiving. The salutation then follows:

> Priest: Peace be with you.
> People: With you and with your spirit.[21]

It is most illuminating to note how this salutation and response were understood by an early theologian within this liturgical tradition. Narsai of Nisibis (died ca. A.D. 502) discusses this point:

Then the priest blesses the people in that hour with that saying which the lifegiving mouth prescribed: 'Peace be with you,' says the priest to the children of the Church, for peace is multiplied in Jesus our Lord who is our peace ...

The people answer the priest lovingly and say: 'With thee, O priest, and with that priestly spirit of thine.' They call 'spirit,' not that soul which is in the priest, but the Spirit which the priest has received by the laying on of hands. By the laying on of hands the priest receives the power of the Spirit, that thereby he may be able to perform the divine Mysteries. That grace the people call the 'Spirit' of the priest, and they pray that he may attain peace with it, and it with him. This makes known that even the priest stands in need of prayer, and it is necessary that the whole Church should intercede for him. Therefore she (the Church) cries out that he may gain peace with his Spirit, that through his peace the peace of all her children may be increased; for by his virtue he greatly benefits the whole Church, and by his depravity he greatly harms the whole community ... 'Peace be with thee,' by whom are celebrated the Mysteries of the Church: 'Peace be to thy Spirit' with thee through thy conduct. 'Peace be with thee,' for great is the deposit[22] entrusted to thee. May the peace of thy Spirit grow through thy diligence in things spiritual.[23]

Narsai understands the words "and with you and with your spirit" in the liturgy of Addai and Mari to indicate that the man to whom they are spoken is one entrusted with the Holy Spirit for the purpose of doing what is given him to do: in this case, celebrating the Lord's Supper. Thus the connection of the Office of the Holy Ministry to the celebration of the Lord's Supper is seen to be absolute. Only one to whom this office has been given can be greeted in this way. Only such a one is to celebrate the Lord's Supper.

One additional piece of evidence may be cited concerning the relation of the Office of the Holy Ministry to the celebration of the Lord's Supper in *Addai and Mari*, namely, the declaration of the priest while distributing the elements:

> *And when the priest gives the body he says*
> The body of our Lord to the discreet priest or to the deacon of God or to the circumspect believer: for the pardon of offences
> *And the deacon says over the chalice*
> The precious blood for the pardon of offences, the spiritual feast for everlasting life to the discreet priest or to the deacon of God *and everyone according to his degree*[24]

Again, it is plain that what is being distributed is "for the pardon of offences," and it is the priest, the holder of the Office of the Holy Ministry, who is entrusted with the distribution of this forgiveness of sins. A deacon assists by giving the cup, but this is done under the oversight of the priest. That the priest is responsible for this means of forgiving and retaining sins may be seen from the fact that he goes first, with the body. He is thus the one who exercises the responsibility for who receives this pardoning of offences and who is denied it.

If Bouyer's theory is correct, then the celebrating priest was the instrument through whom the Lord caused

His words to be spoken. If Bouyer's theory is treated more skeptically, it is still clear that it was left to the priest to say all the prayers which confessed that what was to be celebrated was the Body and Blood of Christ, and that it proclaimed Christ's life, death, and resurrection. It was the priest who prayed that the Lord's Supper celebrated there would be for the forgiveness of those who ate and drank. Even if one were to proceed on the basis of Ratcliff's theory, the conclusion would run from the lesser to the greater: If a priest is necessary to celebrate that which is less than the Lord's Supper, surely it would be necessary that a priest celebrate the Lord's Supper itself. The priest, as has been seen, prayed in the plural; with their "Amen" it was the prayer also of the people. With their response, "with you and with your spirit," they confess him as the one ordained to do what the Spirit's bestowal has put him there to do. In short, the priest—that is, the one ordained into the Office of the Holy Ministry— was the celebrant.

Notes:

[1] Lucien Deiss, Springtime of the Liturgy, trans. Matthew J. O'Connell (Collegeville, MN: The Liturgical Press, 1979), pp. 157-158. Deiss here notes that "Addai and Mari . . . is used by the Nestorians and by the Christians of the Chaldean and Malabar rites who are united with Rome."

Concerning the importance of this liturgy among present day liturgical scholars, Jasper and Cuming offer this observation: "Though known in the West, it was not highly regarded by scholars until E. C. Ratcliff published a seminal article in 1929. Since then, the flow of significant articles has continued unabated at the rate of one about every three years." R. C. D. Jasper and G. J. Cuming, Prayers of the Eucharist, Early and reformed (New York: Pueblo Publishing Company, 1980), p. 39.

[2] Edward C. Ratcliff, "The Original Form of the Anaphora of Addai and Mari: A Suggestion," The Journal of Theological Studies 30 (1929):24-26.

[3] Kenneth Stevenson, "Eucharistic Offering: does Research into Origins make any Difference?," Studia Liturgica 15 (1982/1983):92.

[4] Charles E. Hammond, Liturgies Eastern and Western (London: Oxford University Press, 1878), p. xxii.

[5] Joseph A. Jungmann, The Mass of the Roman Rite: Its Origins and Development, vol. I, trans. Francis A. Brunner (New York: Benziger Brothers, 1951), pp. 40-41. Both the linguistic and the confessional isolation of this liturgical family served to keep its development relatively free of outside influences. Regrettably, the present author is unable to read Syriac, and must therefore rely upon translations of the available material. For a scholarly discussion of the original text, see William F. Macomber, "The Oldest Known Text of the Anaphora of the Apostles," Orientala Christiana Periodica 32 (1966):335-371. The Syriac itself, together with a Latin translation, appears on pp. 358-371. The English translation of Lucien Deiss is based upon this text.

[6] Paul F. Bradshaw, Ordination Rites of the Ancient Churches (New York: Pueblo Publishing Company, 1990), p. 9.

[7] Rudolph Stählin, "Die Geschichte des christlichen Gottesdienstes von der Urkirche bis zur Gaegenwart," in Karl Ferdinand Müller and Walter Blankenburg, eds., Leiturgia, vol. 1 (Kassel: Johannes Stauda Verlag, 1954), p. 31.

[8] F. E. Brightman, Liturgies Eastern and Western, vol. 1, Eastern Liturgies (London: Henry Frowde, 1896), p. 267. One sees here the exclusion from the Anaphora of those who, for whatever reason, are not to receive the body and blood of Christ. The doors were then closed and guarded, resulting in a quite literally "closed" communion. As the priest is entrusted with distributing the forgiveness of sins, so also it was important that the priest not distribute this means of the forgiveness of sins to those who were not to have it. The assistance of the deacons in this matter was here built into the liturgy.

[9] Deiss, p. 159.

[10] Ibid., p. 162.

[11] Macomber's Latin translation reads at this point, ". . . ut sit nobis, Domine, in remissionem debitorum, it veniam peccatorum, . . ." p. 369. Jasper and Cuming (p. 43) offer this translation: ". . . sanctify it, that it may be to us, Lord, for the remission of debts, forgiveness of sins, . . ." In the semitic way, there is apparently no verb such as "win," which seems to have been provided by Deiss in order to make it read more smoothly in translation.

[12] Deiss, p. 163. See Deiss' footnote 17 on this Epiklesis. He observes that there is no prayer that the Holy Spirit would transform the elements, but rather that the Holy Spirit would cause the elements to be beneficially received.

[13] Ibid., p. 163.

[14] See Chapter VI.

[15] Ratcliff, The Original Form, p. 30.

[16] Hans Lietzmann, Mass And Lord's Supper, trans. Dorothea H. G. Reeve (Leiden: E. J. Brill, 1979), p. 417.

[17] Louis Bouyer, Eucharist, trans. Charles Underhill Quinn (Notre Dame,

IN: University of Notre Dame Press, 1968), pp. 151-152. Bouyer suggests the following text (p. 154), based largely on that of Theodore of Mopsuestia: "Our Lord Jesus Christ, together with his apostles on the night he was betrayed, celebrated this great, awesome, holy and divine mystery: taking bread, he blessed it, and broke it, gave it to his disciples and said: This is my body which is broken for you for the remission of sins. Likewise the cup: he gave thanks and gave it to them and said: This is my blood of the New Testament which is shed for many for the remission of sins. Take then all of you, eat of this bread and drink of this cup, and do this whenever you are gathered together in my name."

[18] See in this regard Gregory Dix, The Shape of the Liturgy (London: Dacre Press, 1960), p. 179 (note). Dix points out that "the modern Anglican editors have inserted the narrative of the institution from I Cor. xi. 23-5, apparently because they could not conceive of a eucharistic prayer which did not contain such a feature . . ." He then goes on to point out that there is no manuscript evidence to warrant its insertion, and points to additional historical evidence that it was never part of this liturgy.

[19] Bryan D. Spinks, Addai and Mari—the Anaphora of the Apostles: A Text for Students (Bramcote, GB: Grove Books, 1980), p. 28.

[20] This should not be construed to suggest that the present author believes it to be wise to omit the words that the Lord spoke on the night in which He was betrayed. It would, however, be equally unwise to dismiss this liturgy as providing a rite for a genuine celebration of the Lord's Supper just because the verba are not repeated, or appear not to be.

[21] Deiss, p. 159. Macomber provides a Latin translation, p. 359, and the original Syriac text, p. 358.

[22] A critical edition of the original Syriac text of this homily may be found in Narsai, Homiliæ et Carmina, vol. 1, D. Alphonsi Mingana, ed. (Mausilii: Typis Fratrum Prædicatorum, 1905). According to Mrs. Judith Jones, candidate for the degree of Ph.D. in Biblical Studies with an emphasis in New Testament at Emory University, and Mr. Jeff Kuan, candidate for the degree of Ph.D. in Biblical Studies with an emphasis in History and Archeology at Emory University, no Syriac term corresponding to the English word "deposit" appears in the Syriac text. Mrs. Jones and Mr. Kuan suggest that the Syriac text appears to be corrupt at this point, (line 19, first four Syriac words) but they are unable to determine what evidence the translator had for including the word "deposit" in his translation. Were the uncorrupted text to contain a Syriac word for "deposit," it would be very likely to correspond to the Hebrew. Francis Brown, S. R. Driver, and Charles A. Briggs, Hebrew and English Lexicon (Peabody, MA: Hendrickson Publishers, 1979), p. 786. This term is found in only one chapter of the Old Testament (Gen. 38:17-18, 20), where it refers to Judah's "seal." It was simply transliterated by the Septuagint into Greek as αρραβων, and from

there into Latin as *arrabo*. <u>TWOT</u> 2:393-394. It is an utterly Semitic term, meaning literally a "pledge." St. Paul uses the Greek form of the word in 2 Cor. 1:22. The text reads in English, beginning at verse 21, "Now it is God who makes both us and you stand firm in Christ. He anointed us, set his seal of ownership on us, and put his Spirit in our hearts as a deposit [αρ–ραβωνα], guaranteeing what is to come." In verse 21, St. Paul distinguishes between "us" and "you." When he thus goes on to speak of this αρραβωνα of the Spirit which has been given "us," is he now including the "you" in the "us," thus referring to the deposit of the Spirit bestowed in Holy Baptism (this is clearly the case when he uses the term again in Eph. 1:13-14), or is he maintaining the distinction between "you" and "us," thus referring to an additional deposit of the Spirit given to the Office-holding "us" when they were put into that office? While this question is difficult to answer, Narsai may here be referring to just such a deposit being given to the one who is placed into the Office of the Holy Ministry. The evidence presented earlier might here be rephrased by saying that the reception of one "deposit" of the Holy Spirit for one purpose does not preclude the reception of another "deposit" of the Holy Spirit for another purpose. The Syriac of Narsai is, however, inconclusive on this point. Much more conclusive is the Syriac term which Mrs. Jones and Mr. Kuan identify as meaning "entrusted." From the context, that which is entrusted is the Spirit, and the one who receives that which is being entrusted (the Spirit) is the priest, that is, the one who holds the Office of the Holy Ministry. This works in the way of John 20:21-23, where the Lord is the One who does the entrusting, those who are given the Office of the Holy Ministry are the recipients, and the Holy Spirit is what is entrusted. See 1 Tim. 4:14; 2 Tim. 1:6-7. (See the comments of Holwerda and Scaer, Chapter I).

[23] Narsai, <u>Homilæ et Carmina</u>, *An Exposition of the Mysteries* (Hom. XVII), p. 277. English translation in R. H. Connolly, ed., <u>The Liturgical Homilies of Narsai</u> (London: Cambridge University Press, 1909), pp. 8-9. For biographical information concerning Narsai, see Connolly, pp. ix-xi. For a lengthy argument defending the authenticity of this particular homily, see Connolly, pp. xii-xli. Narsai speaks with unmistakable clarity: "Thus does the Holy Spirit celebrate by the hands of the priest; and without a priest they (sc. the Mysteries) are not celebrated for ever and ever. The Mysteries of the Church are not celebrated without a priest, for the Holy Spirit has not permitted (any other) to celebrate them. The priest received the power of the Spirit by the laying on of hands; and by him are performed all the mysteries that are in the Church ... They that possess not the order cannot celebrate, be they never so just. The righteous cannot by their purity bring down the Spirit; and the sinful by their sinfulness do not hinder His descent." Pp. 287-288, in Connolly, pp. 21-22. One notes here the use of the singular "order." Further there is the confession that the working of

the Holy Spirit is utterly a gift of grace, in no way dependent upon the personal moral condition of the priest. These could serve as the basis for many fruitful paragraphs of commentary, but they are beyond the limitations of the present work. What is important here is that Narsai makes an absolute connection between the Office of the Holy Ministry and the Lord's Supper, and he does so on the basis of the liturgical confession, "And with thy spirit." Robert Cabié comments on the basis of this text:

"'Peace to you' (or 'to all') was the formula used in Antioch and Constantinople. In the West and in Egypt 'The Lord be with you' was also used. The response everywhere was 'And to (or: with) your spirit.' The response, like the celebrant's greeting, was of Semitic origin, and we would expect it to have been translated into Latin and Greek with a simple 'and to (with) you.' That is not what happened, and the reason is to be found in the commentaries of the Fathers: 'He gives the name 'spirit' not to the soul of the priest but to the Spirit he has received through the laying on of hands.'

"The assembly, then, has a celebrant who presides in the name of the Lord; it comes into being in response to a call from God; it is the image of a Church of which Christ, here symbolized by his minister, is the head." Robert Cabié, *The Eucharist*, trans. Matthew J. O'Connell; A. G. Martimort, ed., The Church at Prayer, new ed., vol. 2 (Collegeville, MD: The Liturgical Press, 1986), pp. 50-51.

[24] Brightman, p. 288. The following later reading may be found in The Mar Thoma Syrian Liturgy, trans. George Kuttickal Chacko (New York: Morehouse-Gorham Co., 1956), p. 17:

> Priest: The body of our Lord, sacrificed on
>   Calvary for the forgiveness of sins,
>   the remission of debts and for life
>   eternal, is given to you.
>
> *Communicant*: Amen.
>
> Priest: The blood of our Lord, shed on
>   Calvary for the forgiveness of sins,
>   the remission of debts and for life
>   eternal, is given to you.
>
> *Communicant*: Amen.

CHAPTER XI

THE LITURGY OF SAINT JAMES

The *Liturgy of St. James* belongs to the West Syrian family of liturgies.[1] R. C. D. Jasper and G. J. Cuming suggest that the *Liturgy of St. James* is related to both the *Catecheses* of Cyril of Jerusalem and the *Anaphora of St. Basil*.[2] They date the *Catecheses* to around A.D. 387,[3] and the *Anaphora of St. Basil* to the late third century.[4] It appears to have been translated from the original Greek into Syriac shortly after the Council of Chalcedon (A.D. 451). The Syriac provides the oldest extant version of this liturgy.[5] Louis Bouyer sees the *Apostolic Constitutions* as having exerted an influence upon this liturgy, and comments that "the liturgy of St. James nonetheless remains the most accomplished literary monument of perhaps the whole of liturgical literature."[6]

While clearly being a very ancient liturgy, dating to around the end of the fourth century, it is regrettable that little more than witnesses to the text of the liturgy are available prior to A.D. 800. Jasper and Cuming provide a translation of a ninth century Syriac manuscript, which is used here. They include in brackets those things which appear to have been added by the Greek.[7] Concerning these texts, Bouyer comments:

> . . . the state in which the liturgy of St. James has been handed down to us . . . had already been reached by the middle of the fifth century, for the Syriac translations

used by the "Jacobites" of Syria attest to it in practically all its details.[8]

The very first prayer offered by the priest at the beginning of the divine service is most noteworthy concerning the relation of the Office of the Holy Ministry to the celebration of the Lord's Supper:

> O Sovereign Lord our God, contemn me not, defiled with a multitude of sins: for, behold, I come to this Thy divine and heavenly mystery, not as being worthy; but looking only to Thy goodness, I direct my voice to Thee: God be merciful to me, a sinner; I ... am unworthy to come into the presence of this Thy holy and spiritual table, upon which Thy only-begotten Son, and our Lord Jesus Christ, is mystically set forth as a sacrifice for me ... Wherefore I present to Thee this supplication and thanksgiving, that Thy Spirit the Comforter may be sent down upon me, strengthening me and fitting me for this service; and count me worthy ...[9]

What the holder of the Office of the Holy Ministry undertakes to do, he does only as the Holy Spirit does it through him. As he has received the Holy Spirit at his ordination, so he prays that it would be sent down upon him here, that he would be "strengthened and fitted" (ενισχηον και καταρτηζον) for the doing of that which has been entrusted to him to do in that place, at that time.[10]

The anaphoral section of the communion liturgy begins with a dialog the general contents of which are by now familiar:

The bishop: The love of God the Father, the grace

of our Lord [and] God and Savior Jesus Christ, and
the fellowship [and the gift] of the [all-]Holy Spirit
be with you all.

People: And with your spirit.
The bishop: Let us lift up our minds and our hearts.
People: We have them with the Lord.
The bishop: Let us give thanks to the Lord.
People: It is fitting and right.[11]

The admonition of the bishop, "lift up our minds
and our hearts," is noteworthy, in that it is apparently indicative of this liturgy having borrowed the term "minds" from
the *Apostolic Constitutions* while retaining also "hearts" as it
is found in the *Apostolic Tradition* and other liturgies.[12] The
initial salutation of the bishop is, as in the *Apostolic Constitutions*, taken from 2 Cor. 13:14, and goes beyond the more
modest "the Lord be with you" of the *Apostolic Tradition*. The
response is nevertheless the same, "and with your spirit," a
response which has by now repeatedly been seen to confess
the bestowal of the Spirit upon the one celebrating when he
was placed into the Office of the Holy Ministry.

The bishop then continues with the prayer, "It is
truly fitting and right ...," to which the people respond with
the *Trisagion*. The private prayer of the bishop which follows
recounts the creation, the fall, the giving of the law and the
prophets, and finally the sending of "our Lord Jesus." The
prayer proceeds to recount the events and words of the Lord
"when he was about to endure his voluntary [and life-giving]
death [on the cross,] the sinless for us sinners, in the night
when he was betrayed ..."[13] There follows an embellished
conflation of the institution narratives, in which the bishop
speaks aloud the words of Christ:

(*He stands up, takes the bread, seals it, and says:*) he took bread in his holy, undefiled . . . hands, . . . saying, (*he puts the bread down, saying aloud:*) "Take, eat; this is my body, which is broken and distributed for you for the forgiveness of sins."

People: Amen.

(*He takes the cup, seals it, and says privately:*) "Likewise after supper [he took] the cup . . . , saying, (*he puts it down, saying aloud:*) "Drink from it, all of you; this is my blood of the new covenant, which is shed and distributed for you and for many for the forgiveness of sins." *People:* Amen.[14]

The bishop is here Christ's instrument for the speaking of His words. The people assent to the certainty of what is being done by giving their "Amen." After this, the bishop is also entrusted with praying for the descent of the Holy Spirit upon both the people and the elements:

> *And the bishop stands up and says privately:* . . . and send out upon us and upon these [holy] gifts set before you your [all-]Holy Spirit, . . . (*aloud*) that he may descend upon them, [and by his good and glorious coming may sanctify them,] and make this bread[15] the holy body of Christ, (*People:* Amen.) and this cup the precious blood of Christ. (*People:* Amen.)

> *The bishop stands up and says privately:* that they may become to all who partake of them [for forgiveness of sins and for eternal life] for sanctification of souls and bodies, . . .[16]

A discussion of the implications of such an *Epiklesis*

appearing in the liturgy subsequent to the words of the Lord (*verba*) is beyond the scope of this study. Bryan D. Spinks, not without reason, sees this *Epiklesis* as consecratory.[17] In any case, both the speaking of the *verba* and the praying for the descent of the Holy Spirit are entrusted to the bishop (Greek: Ιερευς = priest), the holder of the Office of the Holy Ministry. The office-holder is the celebrant. He has been given the Spirit for this purpose: he has been spiritually entrusted with the distribution of the forgiveness of sins. That the words, "for the forgiveness of sins," appear to be additions to the Greek text in no way changes this. In either text, it is for "sanctification," and in order to be sanctified (i.e., "made holy"), one's sins must be removed. In any case, the *verba* (to which the people answered with "Amen") clearly and publicly stated that the body and blood of Christ are "distributed . . . for forgiveness of sins."

Intercessory prayer follows. They are spoken by the celebrating bishop (or "priest," as it is in the Greek). He begins with a prayer for the Church, followed by a prayer for the bishops, then for the presbytery, diaconate, and "every ecclesiastical order," then for the priests, then for himself, then the deacons, cities and regions, the emperor, those away from home, the elderly, and so forth.[18] While some doublets occur, there is a generally discernable order to the prayer: first, prayer is offered for the Church, then for bishops, then presbyters, then deacons, and lastly there is prayers which specifically concern the laity. According to the Greek text, in between the prayer for the presbytery (*et al.*) and the prayer for himself, the bishop prays:

> Remember, Lord, the priests who stand around us in this holy hour, before your holy altar, for the offering of the holy and bloodless sacrifice; and give them and

us the word in the opening of our mouths to the glory and praise of your all-holy name.[19]

The explanation of the Lord's Supper as an "unbloody" or "bloodless" (αναιμακτου) sacrifice is one that has already been seen in the *Apostolic Constitutions* to have developed in the region of Antioch. From the context, it is evident that this prayer is offered not on behalf of the "royal priesthood" (i.e., all of the believers there present), but rather for those who hold the Office of the Holy Ministry. The difficulties of "unbloody sacrifice" notwithstanding, the reference is to the celebration of the Lord's Supper. The priests, those who hold the Office of the Holy Ministry, are those who "stand around us . . . for the offering of the . . . sacrifice." There is no indication that anyone else might serve in this capacity.

Finally, as the priest distributes the elements to the people, he says, "to true believers for the pardon of offences and for the remission of sins forever."[20] Here, then, is one last piece of evidence from this liturgy connecting the Office of the Holy Ministry with the celebration of the Lord's Supper. It is the priest who has been given the Spirit for the purpose of forgiving and retaining sins. It is the priest who is entrusted with being the mouthpiece by which the words of the Lord are spoken and the activity of the Holy Spirit upon the elements is solicited. It is, therefore, the holder of the Office of the Holy Ministry who is entrusted with the celebration of the Lord's Supper.

Notes:

[1] Charles E. Hammond, <u>Liturgies Eastern and Western</u> (London: Oxford University Press, 1878), p. xvi.

[2] R. C. D. Jasper and G. J. Cuming, Prayers of the Eucharist, Early and reformed (New York: Pueblo Publishing Company, 1980), p. 88.

[3] Ibid., p. 82.

[4] Ibid., p. 67.

[5] Ibid., pp. 88-89. Spinks argues that the Syriac translation was made before the Council of Chalcedon. Bryan D. Spinks, "The Consecratory Epiklesis in the Anaphora of St. James," Studia Liturgica 11 (1976):22. The Syriac text, set parallel to the Greek text, may be found in Die Syrische Jakobosanaphora, edited by Adolf Rücker (Münster in Westfalen, Germany: Verlag der Aschendorffschen Verlagsbuchhandlung, 1923).

[6] Louis Bouyer, Eucharist, trans. Charles Underhill Quinn (Notre Dame, IN: University of Notre Dame Press, 1968), p. 268.

[7] Jasper and Cuming, p. 88.

[8] Bouyer, p. 277.

[9] "The Divine Liturgy of James, the Holy Apostle and Brother of the Lord," ANF, vol. 7, p. 537. The Greek text of this prayer may be found in F. E. Brightman, Liturgies Eastern and Western, vol. 1: Eastern Liturgies (London: Henry Frowde, 1896), p. 31.

[10] Here, the priest confesses that the reception of the Holy Spirit at his ordination is not an "aorist" action, i.e., it is not something that is done and over with at that time. St. Paul, writing under the inspiration of the Holy Spirit, tells the Ephesians (5:18) to "be filled with the Spirit." The Greek verb used there, πληρουσθε, is a present passive imperative, which can, and in this context does, have continuing force. A Christian, having received the Spirit at Baptism, continues to "be being filled" with the Holy Spirit from then on. So also one who is given the Holy Spirit as he is put into the Office of the Holy Ministry continues to receive the Holy Spirit for that purpose from then on. Thus, one who has received the Holy Spirit for this purpose is here seen to be praying that he would receive the Holy Spirit for that purpose. Keine Mathematik!

[11] Ibid., p. 90. The Greek reads as follows:

Και ο Ιερευς: Η αγαπη του Θεου και Πατρος, η χαρις του Κυριου και Θεου και σωωτηπος ημων Ιησου Χριστου και η κοινωνια και η δωρεα του παναγιου Πνευματος ειη μετα παντων υμων.

Ο Λαος: Και μετα παντων υμων.

Ο Ιερευς: Ανω σχωμεν τον νουν και τα καρδιας.

Ο Λαος: Εχομεν προς τον Κυριον.

Ο Ιερευς: Ευχαριστησωμεν τω Κυριω.

Ο Λαος: Αξιον και δικαιον.

Greek text from Anton Hänggi and Irmgard Pahl, Prex Eucharistica (Fribourg, Switzerland: Éditions Universitaires Fribourg Suisse, 1968), p. 244. (Hereafter PE). These same authors offer a Latin translation of the Syriac of this text on p. 269. The Greek text used here is Vaticanus graecus 2282, which Massey H. Shepherd, Jr., terms "the oldest and best manuscript of the Liturgy of St. James." Massey H. Shepherd, Jr., *Eusebius and the Liturgy of Saint James*, in Yearbook of Liturgical Studies, vol. 4 (Notre Dame, IN: Fides Publishers, 1963), p. 110.

[12] Bouyer, p. 270.

[13] Jasper and Cuming, pp. 90-91.

[14] Ibid., pp. 91-92.

[15] Both here and at the end of this paragraph, Jasper and Cuming observe: "This passage is greatly enlarged in the Syriac." They also note that, while the Greek text is addressed to God the Father, the Syriac version is addressed to Christ. Pp. 92-93, see notes 5, 7. These words appear to draw on Cyril of Jerusalem, *Mystagogical Catecheses* V.7: "Then . . . we call upon the merciful God to send forth His Holy Spirit upon the gifts lying before Him; that He may make [ποιηση] the Bread the Body of Christ, and the Wine the Blood of Christ; for whatsoever the Holy Ghost has touched, is sanctified and changed [μεταβεβληται]." St. Cyril of Jerusalem's Lectures on the Christian Sacraments, edited by F. L. Cross (London: SPCK, 1951), p. 74. For the Greek, see pp. 32-33. Baldovin comments upon this passage: "The explicit notion of change is innovative with regard to the epiclesis. Together with another innovative verb, *poiein* (to make) Cyril signals a shift from previous tradition; i.e. we can now begin to pinpoint a 'moment of consecration.' Explicit focus on such a moment may not have been Cyril's intent, but the wording of the prayer and Cyril's commentary did inspire later Eastern tradition to isolate the epiclesis as the moment of transformation in much the same way the Western tradition concentrated on the words of institution." John F. Baldovin, Liturgy in Ancient Jerusalem (Bramcote: Grove Books, 1989), p. 28. Similarly Dix: ". . . Cyril differs . . . from the whole pre-Nicene church. Serapion follows universal tradition in making the eucharist emphatically an action of Christ . . . But from end to end of Cyril's account of the liturgy and throughout his eucharistic teaching, Christ plays only a *passive* part in the eucharist. He is simply the divine Victim Whose Body and Blood are 'made' by the action of the Holy Ghost, that the earthly church may offer Him to the Father 'in propitiation for our sins'." Gregory Dix, The Shape of the Liturgy (London: Dacre Press, 1960), p. 278. It should be noted, in Cyril's defense, that he does not appear to be submitting a liturgical suggestion here, but rather to be commenting upon how the liturgy as he knows it is done. Even so, it is still apparent that whether it is the Holy Spirit, or Christ, or both that play(s) the active role, the instrument through which the Active One brings about that which is 'in propitiation for our sins' is nevertheless the one who holds the Office of the Holy Ministry.

[16] Jasper and Cuming, p. 93.

[17] Spinks, "The Consecratory Epiklesis," pp. 31-33. In the Greek version, this prayer for the sending of the Holy Spirit occurs yet a second time, as

may be seen in the translation provided by Jasper and Cuming, p. 93, and in the text found in PE, p. 250.

[18] Jasper and Cuming, pp. 94-95.

[19] Ibid., p. 94. For the Greek, see PE p. 252.

[20] Brightman, p. 104.

CHAPTER XII

THE LITURGY OF SAINT MARK

The *Liturgy of St. Mark* developed in Egypt, and is representative of the Alexandrian family of liturgies.[1] R. C. D. Jasper and G. J. Cuming comment,

Our knowledge of the early history of the eucharistic prayer is more detailed for Egypt than for any other area, because of the survival of papyrus and other fragments which have preserved the text in shorter and simpler form than that of the medieval manuscripts, thus giving us a good idea of the eucharistic prayer as it was in the fourth century and earlier.[2]

The earliest evidence available is a single leaf called the *Strasbourg Papyrus*. It appears to have been written between A.D. 300 and 500. Based on certain internal evidence, Jasper and Cuming suggest that the prayer may date back to around A.D. 200.[3]

At a rather early date in the development of the *Liturgy of St. Mark*, it apparently became quite dependent upon the *Liturgy of St. James*. This dependence seems to have grown as time went on and the *Liturgy of St. Mark* continued to borrow from the *Liturgy of St. James*. This is confirmed by a tablet dating from the eighth century containing the second half of the *anaphora of St. Mark*.[4]

After joining in acknowledging the influence of the *Liturgy of St. James*, Jasper and Cuming suggest that the contents of this tablet may be reflective of the liturgical development of *St. Mark* as early as ca. A.D. 400.[5] Based largely, albeit not exclusively, upon a comparison of these two documents, G. J. Cuming draws the following conclusions:

> S[trasbourg] is a Christian *berakah*, a complete anaphora, and possibly dates back to the second century.
>
> The intercessions have always been in their present place and are not an interpolation.
>
> The offering was made in the preface and consisted originally of prayer and thanksgiving, but was later applied to the gifts.
>
> The Sanctus replaced the original doxology, and the rest of the anaphora was built up gradually by additions after the Sanctus.
>
> The intention to 'change' the gifts is a later development, producing the second epiclesis.
>
> The use of the Pauline comment [I Cor. 11:26] to introduce the anamnesis originated in Egypt.[6]

Bryan Spinks has challenged particularly the first point of these conclusions.

> While the possibility that Stras.254 is a complete anaphora cannot be ruled out, the hypothesis cannot yet be taken as proven, and it is premature to place too much weight on it in the reconstruction of the development of the early anaphora.[7]

To summarize, that which is found in this document reliably presents what was the early Alexandrian liturgical practice, but one may not safely assume that what is *not* found in this document was necessarily *not* part of that liturgical practice. The words of institution do not appear. It was nevertheless intended as a celebration of the Lord's Supper, as may be seen by the following words of the text:

> You made everything through . . . your true Son, our Lord and Savior Jesus Christ; giving thanks {[ε] υξαριστουντες} through him to you with him and the Holy Spirit, we offer the reasonable sacrifice and this bloodless service, which all the nations offer you . . .[8]

There is every reason to think that this prayer was prayed by a holder of the Office of the Holy Ministry and no reason to think it was not. In the intercessory section, it is clear that the holders of the Office of the Holy Ministry were entrusted with the offering of the prayers:

> [Remember] our orthodox fathers and bishops everywhere; and grant us to have a part and lot with the fair . . . of your holy prophets, apostles and martyrs. Receive (?) [through] their entreaties [these prayers]; grant them through our Lord, through whom be glory to you to the ages of ages.[9]

At this point, the Strasbourg papyrus is concluded.

The British Museum tablet and the Rylands fragment assume, rather than specifically stating, that a holder of the Office of the Holy Ministry will pray the prayer. The words of institution are included in a form strikingly similar to what is found in the *Liturgy of St. James*. There follows "an explicitly consecratory epiclesis,"[10] which again appears to bear the marks of the influence of the *Liturgy of St. James*.

In the more detailed final form of the *Liturgy of St. Mark*, the relation of the Office of the Holy Ministry to the celebration of the Lord's Supper is made explicit. The bishop

(Greek Ιερευς="priest") begins by praying, as in St. James, a prayer asking the Lord to "enable us in the power of thine Holy Spirit to accomplish this ministry."[11] The bishop/priest is specifically named at the beginning of the *anaphora* as the one who celebrates:

> *Likewise also after the Creed the bishop seals the people, saying aloud:* The Lord be with all.
> *People:* And with your spirit.
> *Bishop:* Up with your hearts.
> *People:* We have them with the Lord.
> *Bishop:* Let us give thanks to the Lord.
> *People:* It is fitting and right.
> *Deacon:* Spread (the fans?)

> *The bishop begins the anaphora:* It is truly fitting and right . . . [12]

Clearly the bishop (or, as the Greek has it, the priest), is the one who invokes the Lord to be with the people, and whom the people acknowledge as having the "spirit" which is placed upon those in the Office of the Holy Ministry. Further comment upon the phrase "and with your spirit" is hardly necessary here. The bishop/priest is the one entrusted with the praying of the anaphoral prayer. The contents of this prayer are very close to the contents of the anaphoral prayer in the *Liturgy of St. James*, and plainly indicate the nature of what has been entrusted to the Office-holding celebrant.

Toward the beginning of the prayer are words quite similar to the earlier version discussed above:

> You made everything through your wisdom, the true light, your only Son, our Lord and God and Savior,

Jesus Christ, through whom with him and the Holy Spirit we give thanks to you and offer this reasonable and bloodless service, which all the nations offer you ...[13]

There follows a section of intercessory prayer much lengthier than that which was recorded in the Strasbourg papyrus. Continuing beyond the point at which the record in that document ends, the final form of the *Liturgy of St. Mark* provides the following:

> *People*: Holy, holy, holy, Lord of Sabaoth; heaven and earth are full of your holy glory.

> *The bishop seals the holy things, saying*: Full in truth are heaven and earth of your holy glory through [the appearing of] our Lord and God and Savior Jesus Christ: fill, O God, this sacrifice also with the blessing from you through the descent of your [all-]Holy Spirit.

> For our Lord and God and King of all, Jesus the Christ, in the night when he handed himself over for our sins, and underwent death [in the flesh] for all men, [sat down with his holy disciples and apostles, he] took bread in his holy, undefiled, and blameless hands, looked up to heaven to you, his own Father, the God [of us and] of all, gave thanks, blessed, sanctified, broke and gave it to his holy and blessed disciples and apostles, saying: (*aloud*) "Take, eat," [*Deacon*: Stretch forth, presbyters.] "this is my body, which is broken for you and given for forgiveness of sins."

> [People: Amen.]

[*The bishop says privately:*] Likewise also after supper he took the cup, he mixed wine and water, [looked up to heaven to you, his own Father, the God of us and of all], gave thanks, blessed, and sanctified it, [filled it with the Holy Spirit,] and gave it to his holy and blessed disciples and apostles, saying: [*aloud*] "Drink from it, all of you;"

[*Deacon:* Still stretch forth.] "this is my blood of the new covenant, which is shed for you and for many, and given for forgiveness of sins."

People: Amen.

[*The bishop prays thus:*] "Do this for my remembrance. For as often as you eat this bread and drink this cup, you proclaim my death and confess my resurrection [and ascension] until I come."[14]

Again, there is a great deal of similarity between these words and those of the *Liturgy of St. James.* As in that liturgy, so also in this one, the fact that the Lord's Supper is for the forgiveness of sins is of such importance that this part of the prayer is spoken aloud, and the people confess the truth of these words with their "Amen." The man who celebrates the Lord's Supper is the man entrusted with the Spirit for the purpose of forgiving and retaining sins, the holder of the Office of the Holy Ministry, the man here called "bishop" or "priest."

There follows, as in *St. James* and in the British Museum tablet, a prayer to the Father that He would,

. . . send out from your holy height . . . the Paraclete

himself, the Holy Spirit . . . upon us and upon these
loaves and these cups . . . (*aloud*) and make the bread
the body (*People*: Amen. [*The bishop, aloud*:]) and the
cup the blood of the new covenant of our Lord and
God and Savior and King of all, Jesus Christ,
[*Deacon*: Descend, deacons; pray, presbyters.] that they
may become to all of us who partake of them for faith,
for sobriety, . . . for forgiveness of sins . . .[15]

As with *St. James*, there is an element of ambiguity
concerning whether the words of the Lord (the *verba*) or
this *Epiklesis* is intended to be understood as responsible
for causing the bread and wine to be the body and blood of
Christ. In either case, however, it is the bishop/priest that
is entrusted with being the instrument through which it is
done. In the *Epiklesis* the bread/body and the wine/blood
are again confessed to be "for forgiveness of sins," the distribution of which has been given with the Spirit by Christ to
the Office of the Holy Ministry.

That the Lord's Supper is truly the body and blood
of Christ, (and is therefore for forgiveness of sins), is further
confessed by the words which the bishop speaks to the communicants during the distribution: "The holy body of our
Lord and God and Savior Jesus Christ. The precious blood
of our Lord and God and Savior Jesus Christ."[16]

It has been seen that in this liturgy, the holders of
the Office of the Holy Ministry celebrate the Lord's Supper. The bishop/priest receives the Holy Spirit for the
purpose of forgiving sins. Because the Lord's Supper is a
means of forgiving sins, the possibility that anyone other
than a bishop/priest would seek to celebrate it is not even
envisioned. Christ gave it to the holy ministry to do. The

146

Holy Spirit works through the holy ministry. Those who hold the Office of the Holy Ministry are entrusted with the forgiving of sins. The celebration of the Lord's Supper is therefore done exclusively by such men.

Notes:

[1] Charles E. Hammond, Liturgies Eastern and Western (London: Oxford University Press, 1878), p. xvi, v.s. p. x.

[2] R. C. D. Jasper and G. J. Cuming, Prayers of the Eucharist, Early and reformed (New York: Pueblo Publishing Company, 1980), p. 52.

[3] Ibid., pp. 52-53. The Greek text of this document, with restored letters in brackets and abbreviations spelled out in parentheses, may be found in PE, pp. 116-119. A Latin translation is included.

[4] Quecke writes concerning the contents of this tablet, "Alle diese Elemente sind den übrigen Zeugen der Markusliturgie mit der Jakobusliturgie gemeinsam und möglicherwiese auch von heir übernommen. Der Einfluß der Jakobusliturgie auf die Markusliturgie ist ein bekannte Tatsache; die Anamnese der melkitisch-griechischen Zeugen der Markusliturgie ist in noch stärkerem Maße von der der Jakobusliturgie abhängig." H. Quecke, "Ein säidischer Zeuge der Markusliturgie (Brit. Mus. Nr. 54036)" Orientalia Christiana Periodica, 37 (1971):50.

[5] The contents of this tablet are confirmed by the sixth century parchment text in the John Rylands Library (the "Rylands fragment"). Jasper and Cuming, pp. 54-55.

[6] G. J. Cuming, "The Anaphora of St. Mark: A Study in Development," Le Muséon 95 (1982):128.

[7] Bryan D. Spinks, "A Complete Anaphora? A Note on Strasbourg Gr.254," The Heythrop Journal 25 (1984):55.

[8] Jasper and Cuming, p. 53. Greek in PE, p. 116.

[9] Jasper and Cuming, p. 54. Greek in PE, p. 118.

[10] Jasper and Cuming, p. 55. For the text, see p. 56. For the Greek, see PE, pp. 120, 122.

[11] F. E. Brightman, Liturgies Eastern and Western, vol. 1, Eastern Liturgies (London: Henry Frowde, 1896), pp. 144(.23)-145.

[12] Jasper and Cuming, p. 59. The Greek reads as follows:
Ομοιως και μετα την πιστιν σφραγιζει ο Ιερευς τον λαον εκφωνων: Ο Κυριος μετα παντων.
Ο Λαως: Και μετα του πνευματος σου.
Ο Ιερευς: Ανω ημων τα καρδιας.
Ο Λαως: Εχομεν προς τον Κυριον.
Ο Διακονο: Πετασατε.

Ο Ιερευς αρχεται της αναφορας: Αληθως γαρ αξιον και δικαιον . . .

Greek text in PE, p. 102. For a Latin translation of the Coptic text, see p. 135.

[13] Jasper and Cuming, p. 59. Greek in PE, p. 102.

[14] Jasper and Cuming, pp. 64-65. The bracketed statements appear in the Greek, but not in the Coptic. Greek in PE, pp. 110, 112.

[15] Jasper and Cuming, pp. 65-66. Greek in PE, p. 114.

[16] Jasper and Cuming, p. 66. Greek in Brightman, p. 140.

CHAPTER XIII

THE LITURGY OF SAINT JOHN CHRYSOSTOM

onstantinople was not as important an early center of Christianity as were Jerusalem, Alexandria, Antioch or Rome. With the moving of the capital of the Empire to Constantinople, however, the city began to fill a very important role within the Church. The impact that Constantinople's rising political position had upon the Church in general, and upon the bishop of that city in particular, is evident from the canons of the Council of Constantinople (A.D. 385)[1] and the Council of Chalcedon (A.D. 451).[2] Constantinople became the center of Byzantine Christianity. Thus, the liturgy of St. John Chrysostom, "became, and has remained, the principle and normal rite of the Orthodox Church, having ousted St. Basil from that position by A.D. 1000."[3] For this reason, a discussion of the Liturgy of St. John Chrysostom is presented here.

Precise dating of the Liturgy of St. John Chrysostom is difficult. While it is generally acknowledged to have been produced subsequent to St. Basil, there are also considerable similarities between it and the Anaphora of the Twelve Apostles, extant only in Syriac.[4] There is debate concerning which of these is dependent upon the other; the possibility that they are both dependent upon yet another, unknown source, has also been advanced. Tied up with this issue is unresolved debate concerning the extent to which the saint whose name it bears was involved in actually authoring the liturgy.[5] If John Chrysostom actually produced it, the liturgy would have originated in the late fourth century.[6] "Chrysostom may have done no more than touch up a liturgy already existing at Antioch which acquired his name when he was transferred to Constantinople."[7]

The text generally used for the study of the Liturgy of St. John Chrysostom is the eighth century Codex Barberinus graecus 336. (This is the text that is used for the present study.) It differs from the present day version only slightly.[8]

There is a Prothesis, but it is less detailed than those of St. James and St. Mark, and it does not contain a petition for the descent of the Holy Spirit upon the celebrant. In the text given by F. E. Brightman, one does find the priest praying that the Lord God would make [ποιησον] the elements into the body and blood of Christ.[9] This prayer was said privately by the priest before the actual beginning of the divine service. Gregory Dix comments:

> And since this [the procession] is the opening of the eucharist proper, the whole centre of gravity of the rite has been shifted back to 'before the liturgy begins'.
>
> But since the eucharist cannot thus have its primary significance transferred to a point before it begins without absurdity, a wholly fresh focus has to be found for it within the rite, and this is found in the 'resurrection' of the 'dead body' of Christ entombed upon the altar.[10]

It may be noted that there are differences in the wording of this prayer among the various manuscripts in which it is recorded.[11] One therefore hesitates to place too great an emphasis upon the precise wording of this Prothesis.

Prior to the beginning of the Anaphora, there is the

kiss of peace, in which the priest speaks peace to the people, who respond "and with your spirit."[12] This having been done, the deacons cry out, "The doors! The doors!," which has been seen to be dismissal of those who are not to be communed, and the closing of the communion. After the Creed, the *Anaphora* begins:

> *The priest says:* The grace of our Lord Jesus Christ, and the love of the God and Father, and the fellowship of the Holy Spirit be with you all.
> *People:* And with your spirit.
> *Priest:* Let us lift up our hearts.
> *People:* We have them with the Lord.
> *Bishop:* Let us give thanks to the Lord.
> *People:* It is fitting and right.[13]

St. Chrysostom here follows the West Syrian liturgies, namely the *Apostolic Constitutions* and *St. James*, in using the longer salutation of 2 Cor. 13:14. It differs only in its more exact quotation of the Holy Scriptures. The response remains what has been seen to be universal: "And with your spirit."

The liturgy then directs the priest to begin the *Anaphora*. After the people have joined in singing the *Trisagion*, the priest continues to pray privately:

> . . . for you so loved the world that you gave your only-begotten Son that all who believe in him may not perish, but have eternal life.

> When he had come and filled all the dispensation for us, on the night in which he handed himself over, he took bread in his holy and undefiled hands, gave

thanks, blessed, broke, and gave it to his holy disciples and apostles, saying, (*aloud*) "Take, eat; this is my body, which is for you." <*privately*> Likewise the cup also after supper, saying, (*aloud*) "Drink from this, all of you; this is my blood of the new covenant, which is shed for you and for many for the forgiveness of sins." *People*: Amen.[14]

This is followed shortly by an *Epiklesis*, which is prayed privately by the priest:

> . . . we pray and beseech and entreat you, send down your Holy Spirit on us and on these gifts set forth; and make [ποιπησον] this bread the precious body of your Christ, Amen; and that which is in this cup the precious blood of your Christ, changing [μεταβαλων] it by your Holy Spirit, Amen . . .[15]

As has been seen in several previous liturgies, the Lord's words are here followed by a prayer that the Holy Spirit would "change" the elements. This would seem to be a bit confusing. Do the Lord's words consecrate the elements, the Holy Spirit working through the words spoken by the Lord? If so, why are these words followed by the *Epiklesis*? Is the Holy Spirit understood here to be changing the elements when invoked to do so in the *Epiklesis*? If so, why are the people silent at this point, their "Amen" having come when the words of the Lord which promised the forgiveness of sins were spoken?[16] In any case, it is clear that the one responsible for the celebration and distribution of this means of the forgiveness of sins is the priest.

The prayers continue. Again the priest prays quietly:

We entrust to You, loving Master, our whole life and hope, and we ask, pray and entreat: make us worthy to partake of your heavenly and awesome Mysteries from this holy and spiritual Table with a clear conscience; for the remission of sins, forgiveness of transgressions, communion of the Holy Spirit, inheritance of the kingdom of heaven, confidence before You, neither to judgment nor to condemnation.[17]

The present-day words of distribution, both those spoken by the priest as he communes himself, and those spoken by him as he communes the congregation, further reinforce the confession that the distribution of the Lord's Supper is, in fact, a distribution of the forgiveness of sins. These words are, however, absent from the ancient text as it is found in Brightman.[18] Nevertheless, the prayer just quoted attests again to the fact that "the remission of sins" and the "forgiveness of transgressions" are distributed in the Lord's Supper, and that by the holders of the Office of the Holy Ministry, just as the Lord has mandated (John 20:22-23).

In this liturgy, one sees that the priest is the one confessed by the people as having been given the Spirit for the purpose of celebrating the Lord's Supper. He is the one who is entrusted with being the means by which the Lord's words are put to the elements, and he is the one entrusted with praying for the descent of the Holy Spirit upon them. There is absolutely no evidence that one who had not been placed into the Office of the Holy Ministry might do these things. The relation between the Office of the Holy Ministry and the celebration of the Lord's Supper is confessed, in this liturgy, to be exclusive.

Notes:

[1] Canon III reads: "The Bishop of Constantinople, however, shall have the prerogative honour after the Bishop of Rome; because Constantinople is New Rome." NPNF 2, 14:178. For Greek and Latin, see Conciliorum Oecumenicorum Decreta, (Bologna, Italy: Instituto per le Scienze Religiose, 1972), p. 32.

[2] Canon XXVIII reads in part: "Following ... the One Hundred and Fifty Bishops beloved of God (who assembled in the imperial city of Constantinople, which is the New Rome ...), we do also enact and decree the same things ... For the Fathers rightly granted privileges to the throne of old Rome, because it was the royal city. And the ... Bishops, actuated by the same consideration, gave equal privileges to the most holy throne of New Rome ..." NPNF 2, 14:287. For Greek and Latin, see Conciliorum, pp. 99-100.

[3] R. C. D. Jasper and G. J. Cuming, Prayers of the Eucharist, Early and reformed (New York: Pueblo Publishing Company, 1980), p. 129. Concerning the differences between St. Basil and St. John Chrysostom, Stählin observes, "Im Grunde handelt es sich um eine einzige Liturgie; denn die beiden Formen unterscheiden sich nicht in der Struktur, sondern nur im Wortlaut der priesterlichen Stillgebete. Die Normalform ist die wohl im 6. Jahrhundert endgültig redigierte Chrysostom-Liturgie ..." Rudolph Stählin, "Die Geschichte des christlichen Gottesdienstes von der Urkirche bis zur Gaegenwart," in Karl Ferdinand Müller and Walter Blankenburg, eds., Leiturgia, vol. 1 (Kassel: Johannes Stauda Verlag, 1954), p. 31. The Liturgy of St. John Chrysostom apparently became dominant because it was shorter.

[4] Jasper and Cuming, pp. 124-125.

[5] Jasper and Cuming, pp. 129-130. A lengthier discussion of the dating of this liturgy may be found in Hans-Joachim Schulz, The Byzantine Liturgy, trans. Matthew J. O'Connell (New York: Pueblo Publishing Company, 1986), pp. 4-10. Schulz appears to suggest a date of the late fourth or early fifth century (pp. 9-10).

[6] Georg Wagner asserts precisely this: that Chrysostom was the author of the liturgy that bears his name. Jasper and Cuming note (p. 130) that his position "has not received much support," particularly as it concerns the relation of the Liturgy of St. John Chrysostom to The Twelve Apostles. Wagner does present a mass of evidence in support of his view that the liturgy was written by Chrysostom, the repetition of which is not possible here. The reader is referred to Georg Wagner, Der Ursprung der Chrysostomusliturgie (Aschendorff, Münster Westfalen, Germany: Aschendorffsche Buchdruckerei, 1973). See especially pp. 6-10, 43-51, 132-133.

[7] Jasper and Cuming, p. 130. For a list of places in the writings of St. John Chrysostom that refer to the liturgy, see Hans Lietzmann, Mass and Lord's Supper, trans. Dorothea H. G. Reeve (Leiden, NL: E. J. Brill, 1979), p. 113;

F. E. Brightman, Liturgies Eastern and Western, vol. 1, Eastern Liturgies (London: Henry Frowde, 1896), pp. 470-481.

[8] Ibid. Jasper and Cuming provide the English translation used here, pp. 131-134. For the full Greek text, see Brightman, pp. 309-344. The Greek text of the Anaphora, together with a Latin translation, may be found in PE 224-229.

[9] For the Greek text, see Brightman, pp. 20-21.

[10] Gregory Dix, The Shape of the Liturgy (London: Dacre Press, 1960), p. 290. Such embellishments of what the Lord instituted notwithstanding, it may still be clearly seen below that what is here celebrated is the Lord's Supper.

[11] Anselm Strittmatter, "'Missa Grecorum.' 'Missa Sancti Iohannis Crisostomi.' The Oldest Latin Version Known of the Byzantine Liturgies of St. Basil and St. John Chrysostom," Traditio 1 (1943):83, note 8.

[12] Brightman, p. 320.
Ο Ιερευς: Ει πηνη πασιν
Ο Λαος: Και τω πνευματι σου.

[13] Jasper and Cuming, p. 131. The Greek, from PE p. 224, reads:
Ο Ιερευς λεγει: Η χαρις του κυριου ημων Ιησου Χριστου και η αγαπη του Θεου και Πατρος και η κοινωνια του αγιου Πνευματος ειη μετα παντων υμων.
Ο Λαος: Και μετα του πνευματος σου.
Ο Ιερευς: Ανω σχωμεν τας καρδιας.
Ο Λαος: Εχομεν προς τον Κυριον.
Ο Ιερευς: Ευχαριστησωμεν τω Κυριω.
Ο Λαος: Αξιον και δικαιον.

[14] Jasper and Cuming, p. 132. For the Greek, see PE, p. 226.

[15] Jasper and Cuming, p. 133. For the Greek, see PE, p. 226.

[16] Timothy Ware explains the present day understanding of the Eastern Church concerning this matter: "According to Latin theology, the consecration is effected by the Words of Institution ... According to Orthodox theology, the act of consecration is not complete until the end of the Epiclesis, and worship of the Holy Gifts before this point is condemned by the Orthodox Church as 'artolatry' (bread worship). The Orthodox, however, do not teach that consecration is effected solely by the Epiclesis, nor do they regard the Words of Institution as incidental and unimportant. On the contrary, they look upon the entire Eucharistic Prayer as forming a single and indivisible whole, so that the three main sections of the prayer—Thanksgiving, Anamnesis, Epiclesis—all form an integral part of the one act of consecration. But this of course means that if we are to single out a 'moment of consecration', such a moment cannot come until the Amen of the Epiclesis." Timothy Ware, The Orthodox Church (New York: Penguin Books, 1964), p. 290. Whether this understanding corresponds to the original intent of the Liturgy of St. John Chrysostom is not certain.

[17] The English translation of the text of this prayer is taken from The Divine

Liturgy of Saint John Chrysostom, trans. Faculty of Hellenic College/Holy Cross Greek Orthodox School of Theology (Brookline, MA: Holy Cross Orthodox Press, 1985), p. 26. (Hereafter "Holy Cross.") The translation was modified slightly by the present author, so that it would agree with the Greek text as it is found in Brightman, p. 338.

[18] Holy Cross, pp. 31-32; Brightman, pp. 341-342.

CHAPTER XIV

THE MOZARABIC LITURGY

T he liturgies analyzed to this point have been largely "Eastern." With the *Mozarabic Rite*, attention is now turned to a "Western" liturgy. The *Mozarabic Rite* belongs to the Gallican liturgical family.[1] Concerning the wide use of liturgies belonging to this family, W. C. Bishop comments:

> In treating the Mozarabic Mass it is impossible to exclude consideration of the Gallican Mass, for this was but a variant of the same rite; and the same may be said of the (original) Celtic Mass. Indeed, this rite (so far as our information goes) seems to have been originally the rite of the whole of the Latin Church, with the exception of the city of Rome and its immediate environs. Even in Africa, the Lectionary which underlies St. Augustine's sermons is clearly of a Gallican and not of a Roman type: the same may be said of the liturgical fragments preserved in quotations; and the only point in which the African liturgy clearly agreed with the Roman against the Gallican was the position of the Pax after the Consecration.[2]

The *Gallican Rite* was completely displaced by the *Roman Rite* by roughly A.D. 800 for a variety of reasons.[3] While the *Mozarabic Rite* bore many similarities to the *Gallican Rite*, it has stood the test of time better than the *Gallican* and the other non-Roman Latin rites of this liturgical family, and has therefore been selected for analysis here. The *Mozarabic Rite*,

. . . was developed in Spain quite early: some masses may be dated c. 400. From 470 Spain was occupied by the Visigoths, who recognized the liturgy as the official rite in 633. The country was occupied by the Arabs from 711 to 1085; hence the name "Mozarabic."[4] The liturgy thus remained in use much later than the Gallican, and is still celebrated in Toledo.[5]

As in other liturgies of the Gallican family, some of the prayers are variable,[6] and the partial text translated in R. C. D. Jasper and G. J. Cuming[7] is but one example. J. P. Migne devotes an entire volume to presenting the various texts of the rite,[8] and D. Marius Férotin has produced two large volumes of *Mozarabic Rite* text and commentary.[9] That which follows is a reconstruction based upon Latin texts which may be found in both of Férotin's volumes and in one other work,[10] and upon the English translation provided by Bishop.[11]

A curious aspect of this liturgy is that the anaphoral section of the liturgy does not appear to be introduced by the nearly universal priestly salutation, "the Lord be with you," followed by the response, "and with your spirit." Instead, one finds the following dialogue:

> *Priest*: I will go to the altar of God:
> *People*: To the God of my joy and gladness.
> *Priest*: Ears to the Lord.
> *People*: We have them with the Lord.
> *Priest*: Up with your hearts.
> *People*: Let us lift them to the Lord.
> *Priest*: To our God and Lord Jesus Christ, Son of God, who is in heaven, let us offer fitting praise and fitting thanks.

People: It is fitting and right.[12]

Upon broader examination of the liturgy, however, it may be seen to be a gross understatement to suggest that those who used it were still familiar with the response, "and with your spirit." It occurs repeatedly throughout the rite.[13] Because it is found at the beginning of the *Missa*,[14] it is seen to be a confession of the Spirit which has been given to him who has been placed there for the celebrating of the Lord's Supper. This is manifestly the case despite the fact that the salutation and response do not occur at the beginning of the dialog where one might normally expect to find them. That this salutation and response occurs shortly after the dismissal of those who are not to receive the Lord's Supper provides further evidence that this is a confession of the Spirit which is given to the holders of the Office of the Holy Ministry for the purpose of forgiving and retaining sins.

Attention is now turned to the service of Holy Communion. After the Dismissal (of those not communicating), there is the Offertory. This is followed by the salutation and response, the *Missa* (the admonition to earnest prayer), and then by several prayers, concluding with prayer for various saints (living and dead, that is, the *Nomina* or "Diptychs,") and a *Post-Nomina* prayer. This is followed by the Peace, which is divided into a prayer for peace, the Grace, the (giving of the) Peace, and the *Antiphon* of peace. Next comes the *Sursum Corda* dialog already quoted, the *Illatio* (or Preface), and the *Sanctus* (or *Trisagion*).[15] At this point, the priest prays the *Post-Sanctus* prayer, the second half of which is the *missa secreta*, an example of which reads as follows:

> . . . for the Lord Jesus [Christ] in the night in which he was betrayed, took bread, giving thanks, brake, and

gave it to them saying, Take and eat, this is my body which is given for you; do this in commemoration of me.[16] Likewise also after supper he took the cup and gave thanks and gave it to them saying, This is the cup of the New Testament in my blood which is poured out for you and for many for the remission of sins: do this as oft as ye drink it in commemoration of me. R. Amen. As often as ye eat this bread and drink this cup ye do show the Lord's death till he come from Heaven in glory. R. So we believe, Lord Jesus.[17]

The priest is the Lord's means, or instrument, for speaking these consecratory words, and the people acknowledge and confess that which has been done with their "Amen." The statement, "So we believe, Lord Jesus," appears to have the effect also of acknowledging and confessing the words spoken by the holder of the Office of the Holy Ministry; in short, it parallels the "Amen."

While the foregoing words to appear to be consecratory, sometimes there is an *Epiklesis* which follows in the *Post Pridie.* One example of this kind of prayer reads as follows:

We therefore thy servants beseech thee that thou wouldest sanctify this oblation by the infusion of thy Spirit and fully transform it into the body and blood of our Lord Jesus Christ : that we may be made meet to be cleansed from the stain of our offences by that victim whose redemption of us we celebrate . . . R. Amen.[18]

Concerning such prayers, A. A. King comments that

The place and function of the prayer as *confirmatio*

Sacramenti gives ample opportunity for the prolixity of the Spanish fathers. The definition of the prayer might seem to suggest that St. Isidore regarded it as an epiclesis needed to complete the consecration, but elsewhere he speaks of *Verba Dei...scilicet: Hoc est corpus meum* as the *substantia Sacramenti*. The assumption that an invocation of the Holy Spirit subsequent to the recital of the words of institution is an indispensable element in the liturgy is by no means primitive. The theory was adopted by the Byzantines for propaganda purposes.[19]

He goes on to point out evidence found in one of the *Post Pridie* prayers that the *verba* effected the consecration,[20] and notes that while some of the prayers contain "an unmistakable invocation of the Holy Spirit," in others this is not so clear.[21] The point is that apparently only the *verba*, and not an *Epiklesis*, appear to be necessary for the consecration of the elements.

The priest, that is, the holder of the Office of the Holy Ministry, was the one who was repeatedly confessed by the congregation to have been given the spirit for the purpose of doing what such office-holders do; that is, forgiving and retaining sins.[22] This confession, "and with your spirit," is made at the completion of this prayer, once immediately prior to the distribution, and once between those two points.[23] Even if one were to argue that the *Epiklesis* was understood to effect the consecration in this liturgy, this would do little to change the understanding of the relation of the Office of the Holy Ministry to the celebration of the Lord's Supper. In asking "why" only those who had been entrusted with the Office may celebrate the Lord's Supper, the emphasis might be switched from the fact that Christ has mandated only to such men to be His instruments for speaking these words (Matt. 26:20, 26-28, 1 Cor. 11:24-25, see the discussion of ποιειν in Chapter IV), to the fact that Christ has promised the Holy Spirit's sin forgiving operation only through such men (John 20:21-23). In either case, the understanding and the liturgical confession that only holders of the Office of the Holy Ministry are to celebrate the Lord's Supper remains unchallenged.

Notes:

[1] The reader is cautioned that liturgiologists refer to the Gallican family as including the *Gallican, Mozarabic, Ambrosian,* and *Celtic* rites. Care must be exercised not to confuse the Gallican family with the *Gallican Rite*, the later being but one of several members of the former.

[2] W. C. Bishop, The Mozarabic and Ambrosian Rites, edited by C. L. Feltoe (Milwaukee: The Morehouse Publishing Co., 1924), p. 20, note 1. This same author has compiled a mass of evidence, mostly from the writings of St. Augustine, but also from other African authors, demonstrating that the African Rite more closely resembled liturgies of the Gallican family than the *Roman Rite.* This is not particularly surprising, especially considering St. Augustine's close acquaintance with St. Ambrose of Milan. W. C. Bishop, "The African Rite," Journal of Theological Studies 13 (1911-1912):250-277. Citations of "Bishop" in the following notes refer to the former of these two works.

[3] R. C. D. Jasper and G. J. Cuming, Prayers of the Eucharist, Early and reformed (New York: Pueblo Publishing Company, 1980), p. 147. See also Bard Thompson, Liturgies of the Western Church (Philadelphia: Fortress Press, 1961), pp. 28-30. He writes: "The Gallic type could not withstand the tide of history . . . In the Frankish kingdom its demise was most pronounced. There it had no regulating center and, consequently, no controlled development; but it spun out diverse forms that suffered by comparison to the sober and orderly character of Roman worship. In fact, elaboration was the chief temptation of the Gallic type everywhere. The liturgies . . . abounded in variable elements to such an extent that virtually every feast day was fitted out with its own distinctive formulary." Pp. 29-30. The reader is left with this historical example to draw conclusions for himself concerning the wisdom of creating "liturgies" for each Sunday service.

[4] Literally, "arabized."

[5] Jasper and Cuming, p. 151.

[6] Ibid., p. 147.

[7] Ibid., pp. 152-154. No indication is given as to the Latin source of the English translation presented here.

[8] *Liturgia Mozarabica*, in J. P. Migne, ed., Patrologiæ, Series Latina (Paris, 1862), vol. 85.

[9] *Le Liber Ordinum en Usage Dans l'Eglise Wisigothique et Mozarabe d'Espagne*, edited by D. Marius Férotin, Monumenta Ecclesiae Liturgica, vol. 5 (Paris: Librairie de Firmin-Didot, 1904), hereafter "*Lib. Ord.*" *Le Liber Mozarabicus Sacramentorum et les Manuscrits Mozarabes*, edited by D. Marius Férotin, Monumenta Ecclesiae Liturgica, vol. 6 (Paris: Librairie de Firmin-Didot, 1912), hereafter "*Lib. Moz.*"

[10] Concelebratio Eucharistica Ritu Hispano Veteri Seu Mozarabico (Salamanca, Spain: Calatrava, 1976).

[11] Bishop, pp. 27-45.

[12] Jasper and Cuming, p. 152. The Latin may be found in Concelebratio Eucharistica, pp. 76-77:

> V : *Introibo ad altare Dei.*
> R : *Ad Deum qui laetificat juventutem meam.*
> V : *Aures ad Dominum.*
> R : *Habemus ad Dominum.*
> V : *Sursum corda.*
> R : *Levemus ad Dominum.*
> V : *Deo ac Domino nostro Jesu Christo, Filio Dei, qui es in coelis, dignas laudes dignasque gratias referamus.*
> R : *Dignum et justum est.*

[13] The only difference in wording between the Mozarabic usage and that which has been seen previously is that the Latin adds the word "*semper*" to the salutation, "*Dominus sit semper vobiscum*," that is, "The Lord be *always* with you." The response remains as before, "*Et cum spiritu tuo*," "And with your spirit." This salutation and response is found at the conclusion of the Introit (Concelebratio Eucharistica, p. 60), immediately prior to the Old Testament reading (p. 65), prior to the Psalm (p. 65), prior to the Gospel (p. 67), and immediately following the Sermon (p. 68). At that point the Catechumens, Penitents, and others who were not to receive the Lord's Supper were dismissed. It was at this point that the Missa actually began, and again one finds this salutation and response (p. 72). The dialog mentioned above is found prior to the preface. Between the breaking of the bread and the Creed the salutation and response is found again (p. 80), also prior to the blessing (p. 84), prior to the communing of the priest (p. 85), after the communion and before the post-communion collect (p. 86), and finally, just prior to the Dismissal (p. 87).

[14] Ibid., p. 72.

[15] Examples of the Latin text of this section of the Divine Service may be

found in <u>Concelebratio Eucharistica</u>, pp. 63-78; <u>Lib. Ord.</u>, cols. 229-238; and <u>Lib. Sac.</u>, cols. 620-622. Jasper and Cuming, pp. 152-153, provide an outline of the service. The English text of this section of the Service may be found in Bishop, pp. 27-38.

[16] Jasper and Cuming record an "Amen" of the people at this point.

[17] The English translation may be found in Bishop, pp. 38-39. This is a translation of the text found in <u>Lib. Sac.</u>, col. 327, note: "*Quoniam Dominus Jesus Christus in qua nocte tradebatur accepit panem, gratias agens, fregit et dixit : Accipite et manducate, hoc est corpus meum quod pro uobis tradetur, hoc facite in meam commemorationem. Similiter et calicem postquam cenauit accepit et gratias egit et dedit illis, dicens : Hic calix nouum testamentum in meo sanguine, qui pro uobis et pro multis effundetur in remissione peccatorum : cumque biberitis hoc facite in meam commemorationem. Amen. Quotienscumque panem istum manducaueritis et calicem biberitis, mortem Domini adnuntiabitis donec ueniat. In claritatem e celis. Sic credimus, Domine Ihesu.*"

[18] English in Bishop, p. 39. The Latin is from <u>Lib. Sac.</u>, col. 622.35: "*Ob hoc ergo, quesumus famulantes, ut oblationem hanc Spiritus tui Sancti permixtione sanctifices, et corporis ac sanguinis Ihesu Christi Filii tui plena transfiguratione confirmes. — Vt hostia, qua nos redemptos esse meminimus, . . . Amen.*" A similar prayer may be found in <u>Concelebratio Eucharistica</u>, p. 79.

[19] Archdale A. King, <u>Liturgies of the Primatial Sees</u> (Milwaukee: The Bruce Publishing Company, 1957), pp. 609-610.

[20] See the prayer for the fourth Sunday after the Octave of Easter in <u>Lib. Sac.</u>, col. 313.2. The first half of the prayer reads: "*Hec pia, hec salutaris hostia, Deus Pater, qua tibi reconciliatus est mundus. Hoc est corpus illud, quod pependit in cruce. Hic etiam sanguis, qui profluxit ex latere.*"

[21] A. A. King, p. 610.

[22] One finds further evidence that the distribution of the Lord's Supper is a means of distributing the forgiveness of sins in the Mozarabic words of distribution following a Baptism: "*Corpus Domini nostri Ihesu Christi sit salbatio tua.*" ("The body of our Lord Jesus Christ be your salvation.") "*Sanguis Christi maneat tecum, redemtio tua.*" ("The blood of Christ remain with you as true redemption.") <u>Lib. Ord.</u>, col. 35, note 1; Jasper and Cuming, p. 154. Where there is salvation/redemption, there one necessarily finds also the forgiveness of sins (Luther, <u>Small Catechism</u>, p. 21. <u>BKS</u>, p. 520). See <u>Ordo Antiquus Gallicanus</u>, edited by Klaus Gamber (Regensburg: Verlag Friedrich Pustet, 1965), p. 38, for a Latin text in which it is explicit that the priest (*sacerdos*) was the one who prayed both the *verba* and the *Post Pridie* in the *Mozarabic Rite* of the sixth century.

[23] Bishop, pp. 40-43. <u>Concelebratio Eucharistica</u>, pp. 80-85. Between the *Post Pridie* and the Distribution, one finds the Creed, the Lord's Prayer, and a blessing.

CHAPTER XV

THE MASS OF THE ROMAN RITE

Particularly for the history of the Church in the West, the *Mass of the Roman Rite* stands unchallenged as the most important liturgy. For this reason, one regrets all the more that its origins remain obscure. Joseph A. Jungmann comments:

> The beginnings of the Latin Mass in Rome are wrapped in almost total darkness. The oldest documents to register such a Mass are nearly all the work of diligent Frankish scribes of the eighth and ninth centuries, and even with all the apparatus of literary criticism and textual analysis, we can hardly reconstruct any records back beyond the sixth century, certainly not beyond the fifth.[1]

Be this as it may, the same author considers the available evidence from that *terminus* on to be quite reliable:

> Only the following parts of our Roman canon could not be found at the beginning of the fifth century: *Communicantes, Hanc igitur,* and after the consecration, *Memento etiam* and *Nobis quoque.* However, these formulas too (with the exception of the *Memento* for the dead), are to be found in the oldest manuscripts of the Roman canon, in a form that must at all events belong to the sixth century. During the interval all these prayers came into being; and the others took on,

where they differed, the form they have at present.[2]

By the time of the Lutheran Reformation, a number of corruptions had crept into the *Roman Rite*. A liturgical reform occurred within the Roman Church shortly after that time. Bard Thompson explains:

> The liturgical commission appointed by Pius IV (d. 1565) completed its work under his successor. By the Bull, *Quo primum tempore* of July 14, 1570, the *Missale Romanum* of Pius V was imposed upon all priests and congregations of the Latin rite. ... there are many indications that the commission meant to recover the ancient rite, disengaging it from all accretions of Franko-German origin that distorted its primitive shape ... It is apparent that the new Missal fell short of the mark ... Nevertheless, the amount of purification was appreciable.[3]

Concerning particularly the Canon, Ralph A. Keifer pointedly states, "The form of the Roman Canon now known to Roman Catholics as Eucharistic Prayer I has continued in use virtually unaltered (aside from very minor revisions) from the sixth century to the present day."[4]

One is not able with certainty to date the *Roman Canon* back as early as some of the other rites that have been seen previously. Further, due to its growth, diversity, and fluctuation, it is nearly impossible to identify a single, early, pristine form. Still, its general structure and content are quite ancient, and is certainly not to be dismissed as a mere Roman reaction to the Lutheran Reformation. The same author writes:

. . . the redactors of the Roman Canon were not haphazard or unselective with regard to the materials which they placed in the first part of the eucharistic prayer. Granting the underlying presuppositions, praise-oblation, and oblation-offering *for* something or someone, everything else falls into place. Whether the resulting pattern of eucharistic prayer is found appealing or not is open to question, but it cannot be denied that on its own ground it is coherent.[5]

For these reasons, it appears best to proceed primarily with an analysis of the *Mass of the Roman Rite* as it presently stands, rather than attempting to engage in conjectural reconstruction of a more primitive form. Evidence that is clearly of a later origin will not be brought forward for primary consideration.

Before proceeding directly into a consideration of the *Mass*, however, consideration is first given to a most helpful piece of information concerning both the contents of the Roman Canon in general and the understanding of the relation of the Office of the Holy Ministry to the celebration of the Lord's Supper in particular. This comes in the form of a late fourth century work by St. Ambrose entitled *De Sacramentis*:

> You perhaps say: 'My bread is usual.' But that bread is bread before the words of the sacraments; when consecration has been added, from bread it becomes the flesh of Christ. So let us confirm this, how it is possible that what is [*est*][6] bread is the body of Christ.
>
> By what words, then, is the consecration and by whose expressions? By those of the Lord Jesus. For all the rest that are said in the preceding are said by

the priest: praise to God, prayer is offered, there is a petition for the people, for kings, for the rest. When it comes to performing a venerable sacrament, then the priest uses not his own expressions, but he uses the expressions of Christ. Thus the expression of Christ performs this sacrament.

What is the expression of Christ? Surely that by which all things were made ...

Therefore, to reply to you, there was no body of Christ before the consecration, but after the consecration I say to you that now there is the body of Christ. He himself spoke and it was made; He Himself commanded and it was created.[7]

It may be seen from this text that the so-called "eucharistic prayer" proceeded in a manner similar to that of the *Roman Canon*. Keifer comments:

> Evidently, then, the eucharistic prayer known to Ambrose began with praise followed by intercessions, followed in turn by the institution narrative (*utitur sermonibus Christi*). At least in broad outline, the sixth century Canon shows the same sequence. The *Vere dignum-Sanctus* would be aptly described as *laus deo*, and the *Te igitur-Hanc igitur* could be described as *oratio-petitio*.[8]

St. Ambrose stresses here that the priest is but the instrument through which Christ expresses, by means of His creative word, that the bread is His body. There is no suggestion that the priest is in any way to be seen as the doer of it, nor is there a hint that he wields some sort of special power in this regard. What is done is Christ's doing, and it is done by the speaking of his words. Nevertheless, the priest is explicitly named as the one who serves Christ as His instrument. That the rite being described by St. Ambrose was quite similar to the *Canon of the Roman Mass* may be seen from his quotation of the Divine Service with which he was familiar:

> Do you wish to know how it is consecrated with heavenly words? Accept what the words are. The priest speaks. He says: 'Perform for us this oblation written, reasonable, acceptable, which is a figure of the body and blood of our Lord Jesus Christ. On the day before He suffered He took bread in His holy hands, looked toward heaven, toward you, holy Father omnipotent, eternal God, giving thanks, blessed, broke, and having broken it gave it to the Apostles and His disciples, saying: "Take and eat this, all of you; for this is my body, which shall be broken for many".' Take note.
>
> 'Similarly also, on the day before He suffered, after they had dined, He took the chalice, looked toward heaven, toward thee, holy Father omnipotent, eternal God and giving thanks He blessed it, and gave it to the Apostles and His disciples, saying: "Take and drink of this, all of you; for this is my blood".' Behold! All of these words up to 'Take' are the Evangelist's, whether body or blood. From them on the words are Christ's: 'Take and drink of this, all of you; for this is my blood.'
>
> ... before the words of Christ, the chalice is full of wine and water; when the words of Christ have been added, then blood is effected, which redeemed the people ...
>
> ... he who ate the manna died; he who has eaten this body will effect for himself remission of sins and

'shall not die forever.'⁹

The similarity of the words quoted above and below to those of the *Canon of the Mass* are pronounced. A few lines later, St. Ambrose continues:

> And the priest says: 'Therefore, mindful of His most glorious passion and resurrection from the dead and ascension into heaven, we offer you this immaculate victim, a reasonable sacrifice, an unbloody victim, this holy bread, and chalice of eternal life. And we ask and pray that you accept this offering upon your sublime altar through the hands of your angels, just as you deigned to accept the gifts of your just son Abel and the sacrifice of our patriarch Abraham and what the highest priest Melchisedech offered you.'
>
> So, as often as you receive, what does the Apostle say to you? As often as we receive, we proclaim the death of the Lord. If death, we proclaim the remission of sins [*remissionem peccatorum*]. If, as often as blood is shed, it is shed for the remission of sins, I ought always accept Him, that He may always dismiss my sins. I, who always sin, should always have a remedy.¹⁰

St. Ambrose here explains that to receive the Lord's Supper is to proclaim and "accept" (the same verb is translated "receive" twice previously in this paragraph) the remission of sins. Jungmann comments on the texts cited above that Ambrose "is trying to show his listeners that it is Christ's creative word which turns the earthly gifts into the Lord's Body and Blood," and then observes:

> …we must accept this as certain: the core of our Mass

canon, from the *Quam oblationem* on, including the sacrificial prayer after the consecration, was already in existence by the end of the fourth century. We do not know for sure whether the slight differences in wording are to be traced to a divergent older text or are to be charged to the episcopal orator who, to be sure, was really concerned only with the words of consecration.[11]

This 'Ambrosian' introduction to the *Canon of the Roman Mass* may be concluded with the following observations: 1) The present text of the *Canon* appears to have considerable precedent in the late fourth century, as attested by St. Ambrose. 2) This is particularly true of the verba, which were already at that time understood to be spoken by Christ as at the Last Supper, and to be consecratory. 3) While Christ was understood to cause the bread and wine to be His body and blood by means of His consecratory verba, it is evident that Christ's instrument for speaking His verba was always a priest, that is, a holder of the Office of the Holy Ministry. The words of Christ effected the presence of His body and blood, but Christ spoke them by way of the mouth of one whom He had entrusted with the speaking of them. It went without saying that none of the faithful would presumptuously arrogate to himself the doing of something that Christ had not entrusted him with doing.

This fourth century historical background having been noted, we turn now to the text of the *Mass of the Roman Rite* itself. The following outline of the Divine Service is provided by Jasper and Cuming:

Psalm 43
Confession and Absolution

Introit Psalm
Kyrie
Gloria in Excelsis
Collect of the Day
Epistle
Gradual and Sequence
Gospel
Sermon
Creed
Offertory Prayers
The Canon
Lord's Prayer, Embolism, Fraction
Communion Prayers
Communion
Post-Communion Prayer
Dismissal[12]

While useful consideration of the relation of the Office of the Holy Ministry to the forgiveness of sins might result from an examination of the confession and absolution section, the real evidence concerning the relation of this office to the celebration of the Lord's Supper is to be found in the Offertory Prayers and in the Canon itself. Following the Creed, the priest says to the people:

Priest: The Lord be with you.
People: And with your spirit.
Priest: Let us pray.

Holy Father, almighty, everlasting God, accept this unblemished sacrificial offering, which I, thy unworthy servant, make to thee, my living and true God, for my countless sins, offences and neglects, and on behalf of all who are present here; likewise for all believing Christians, living and dead. Accept it for their good and mine, so that it saves us and brings us to everlasting life. Amen.[13]

Here again one sees the confession that the priest is one into whom the Spirit has been placed for the purpose of forgiving sins ("and with your spirit"), and so he is entrusted specifically and spiritually with the celebration of the Lord's Supper.[14] That which is here to be celebrated is "for . . . sins, offences and neglects"; that is, for their forgiveness. That which is being done is pointedly located in the celebrating priest, "which I . . . make . . ." As this prayer continues, the Holy Spirit is invoked: "Come, thou sanctifier, almighty, everlasting God, and bless these sacrificial gifts, prepared for the glory of thy holy name."[15]

While this prayer is spoken by the priest, it is plainly not consecratory. The Holy Spirit is asked to "bless" (not "change") the elements, and this prayer is made prior to the speaking of the *verba* and, in fact, prior even to the beginning of the Preface to the Canon. This prayer is therefore not to be equated with an eastern *Epiklesis*.

At the conclusion of the Offertory Prayers, the Preface to the Canon begins:

> *Priest*: The Lord be with you.
> *People*: And with your spirit.
> *Priest*: Up with your hearts.
> *People*: We have them with the Lord.
> *Priest*: Let us give thanks to the Lord our God.
> *People*: It is fitting and right.[16]

This Preface, or something very much like it, has been seen in every liturgy that has been examined to this

174

point. The people acknowledged by their "and with your spirit" that the celebrant has been entrusted by Christ with the celebration of the Lord's Supper, at which point the priest proceeds to pray the Prefatory Prayer. The people respond with the *Trisagion*. Then, the priest begins to pray the Canon, which consists of twelve parts. Several of those parts, roughly in the middle of the Canon, are particularly pertinent to this study:

Priest: *Te igitur*—

Memento Domine—

Communicantes—

Hanc igitur—

Quam oblationem—Vouchsafe, we beseech you, O God, to make this offering wholly blessed, approved, ratified, reasonable, and acceptable; that it may become to us the body and blood of your dearly beloved Son Jesus Christ our Lord;

Qui pridie—who, on the day before he suffered, took bread in his holy and reverend hands, lifted up his eyes to heaven to you, O God, his almighty father, gave thanks to you, blessed, broke, and gave it to his disciples, saying, "Take and eat from this, all of you; for this is my body." Likewise after supper, taking also this glorious cup in his holy and reverend hands, again he gave thanks to you, blessed and gave it to his disciples, saying, "Take and drink from it, all of you; for this is the cup of my blood, of the new and eternal covenant, the mystery of faith, which will be shed for you and for many for forgiveness of sins. As often as you do this, you will do it for my remembrance."

Unde et memores—

Supra quae—

Supplices te—
Memento etiam—
Nobis quoque—
Per quem—[17]

The likeness of the part of the *Canon* quoted above, as well as the next three parts (the *Unde et memores, Supra quae,* and *Supplices te*), to the text found in St. Ambrose is most noteworthy. With a few minor changes in wording, this section of the prayer is clearly ancient. The speaking of Christ's *verba* consecrates the elements, causing the bread and wine to be His body and blood. His *verba* specifically state that this is for the forgiveness of sins. The instrument which Christ uses to speak these words is an ordained holder of the Office of the Holy Ministry; that is, a priest.

Following the Canon one finds the Lord's Prayer, Embolism, and Fraction. At this point the priest says, "The peace of the Lord be always with you." The people respond, "And with your spirit."[18] The *Agnus Dei* follows shortly, further reinforcing the confession that the body and blood of Christ "take away the sins of the world." During the distribution, the priest speaks the words, "The Body of our Lord Jesus Christ preserve your soul for everlasting life. Amen."[19] As the service concludes, the salutation of the priest, "the Lord be with you," and the response of the people, "and with your spirit," is found several more times.[20] These rubrics further reinforce the liturgical confession that what is being celebrated is the Lord's Supper, that it is for the forgiveness of sins, and that the one entrusted with the Holy Spirit for the forgiving of sins is the priest, the holder of the Office of the Holy Ministry.

176

Notes:

[1] Joseph A. Jungmann, The Mass of the Roman Rite: Its Origins and Development, vol. 1, trans. Francis A. Brunner (New York: Benziger Brothers, 1951), p. 49. So also Rudolph Stählin, "Die Geschichte des christlichen Gottesdienstes von der Urkirche bis zur Gaegenwart," in Karl Ferdinand Müller and Walter Blankenburg, eds., Leiturgia, vol. 1 (Kassel: Johannes Stauda Verlag, 1954), p. 36: "Die Geschichte des römischen Ritus in den Jahrhunderten nach Hippolyt liegt völlig im Dunkel. Erst im fränkischer Zeit haben wir wieder ein genaues Bild der liturgischen Verhältnisse."

[2] Jungmann, vol. 1, p. 55. For a detailed comparison of early texts of the Canon, see Edmund Bishop, "On the Early Texts of the Roman Canon," Journal of Theological Studies 4 (1903):555-577.

[3] Bard Thompson, Liturgies of the Western Church (Philadelphia: Fortress Press, 1961), pp. 47-48. "The present text of the Canon has been fairly uniform since about 700, but we have insufficient evidence to be able to say what its precise forms were between 350-70, when it seems to have come into existence, and 700." G. G. Willis, Essays in Early Roman Liturgy (London: S.P.C.K., 1964), p. 121.

[4] Ralph A. Keifer, "The Unity of the Roman Canon: An Examination of its Unique Structure," Studia Liturgica 11 (1976):39.

[5] Ibid., p. 55.

[6] By his use of the present tense, St. Ambrose confesses that the consecrated host is in fact both the body of Christ and bread; it neither fails to become Christ's body, nor does it cease to be bread.

[7] Ambrose, De Sacramentis, IV.14-16. English text in Saint Ambrose: Theological and Dogmatic Works, trans. Roy J. Deferrari, The Fathers of the Church, vol. 44 (Washington, D. C.: The Catholic University of America Press, 1963), pp. 302-303; hereafter Fathers 44. For the Latin (with a French translation), see Ambroise de Milan: Des Sacraments, Des Mystères, trans. Bernard Botte, Sources (1961) 25:108-111.

[8] Keifer, p. 41.

[9] Ambrose, De Sacramentis IV.21-24. English: Fathers 44, pp. 304-305. Latin: Sources 25:114-117. The Latin reads in part: "Dicit sacerdos : Fac nobis, inquit, hanc oblationem scriptam, rationabilem, acceptabilem, quod est figura corporis et sanguinis domini nostri Iesu Christi. Qui pridie quam pateretur, in sanctis manibus suis accepit panem, respexit ad caelum, ad te, sancte pater omnipotens aeterne deus, gratias agens bene-dixit, fregit, fractumque apostolis et discipulis suis tradidit dicens : Accipite et edite ex hoc omnes, hoc est enim corpus meum quod pro multis confringetur.

"Similiter etiam calicem postquam cenatum est, pridie quam pateretur, accipit, respexit ad caelum ad te, sancte pater omnipotens aeterne deus, gratias agens benedixit, apostolis et discipulis suis tradidit dicens : Accipite et bibite ex hoc omnes, hic est enim sanguis meus."

[10] Ibid., IV.27-28. English: <u>Fathers</u> 44, p. 306; Latin: <u>Sources</u> 25:116-119. The first of these two paragraphs reads in the Latin: *"Et sacerdos dicit : Ergo memores gloriosissimae eius passiones et ab inferis resurrectionis et in caelum ascensiones, offerimus tibi hanc immaculatam hostiam, ratioabilem hostiam, incruentam hostiam, hunc panem sanctum et calicem vitae aeternae, et petimus et precamur uti hanc oblationem suscipias in sublime altare tuum per manus angelorum tuorum, sicut suscipere dignatus es munera pueri tui iusti Abel et sacrificium patriarchae nostri Abrahae et quod tibi obtulit summus sacerdos Melchisedech."*

[11] Jungmann, vol. 1, pp. 52-53.

[12] R. C. D. Jasper and G. J. Cuming, <u>Prayers of the Eucharist, Early and reformed</u> (New York: Pueblo Publishing Company, 1980), pp. 162-167.

[13] Both the English and the Latin may be found in Thompson, pp. 64-65. The present author has modified the English found there where such modification seemed warranted. For example, the Latin *"Et cum spiritu tuo"* was blatantly mistranslated with the banality "And with you." Such errors are not finally to be laid at Thompson's feet, as he claims to present a transcription of the text in *"The Missal in Latin and English*, being the text of the *Missale Romanum* with English rubrics and a new translation (Westminster: Newman Press, 1959), pp. 676-720" (p. 91). The present author has not been able to lay his hands on a copy of this volume. The Latin text is provided, so that the reader may check it against other mistranslations that the present author may not have corrected:

"Dominus vobiscum.

    Et cum spiritu tuo.

    Oremus. Suscipe, sancte Pater, omnipotens aeterne eus, hanc immaculatam hostiam, quam ego indignus famulus tuus offero tibi Deo meo vivo et vero, pro innumerabilibus peccatis, et offensionibus, et negligentiis meis, et pro omnibus circumstantibus, sed et pro omnibus fidelibus christianis vivis atque defunctis: ut mihi et illis proficiat ad salutem in vitam aeternam. Amen."

[14] One could write at length concerning the reference to the Lord's Supper as a "sacrificial offering," that this is distortion of what was entrusted by the Lord to the apostles, etc. While this could be a most worthy point of further consideration, it is beyond the scope of this work to engage this point.

[15] Thompson, pp. 66-67. The Latin reads: *"Veni, sanctificator, omnipotens aeterne Deus: et benedic hoc sacrificium, tuo sancto nomini praeparatum."*

[16] English text in Jasper and Cuming, p. 163. The Latin may be found in Thompson, p. 68:

    C. *Dominus vobiscum.*

    R. *Et cum spiritu tuo.*

    C. *Sursum corda.*

    R. *Habemus ad Dominum.*

    C. *Gratias agamus Domino Deo nostro.*

    R. *Dignum et justum est.*

178

[17] Jasper and Cuming, pp. 164-165. The Latin of these two sections, as well as the next three (provided for purposes of comparison with St. Ambrose) reads: *"Quam oblationem tu, Deus, in omnibus, quaesumus, benedictam, adscriptam, ratam, rationabilem, acceptabilemque facere digneris: ut nobis Corpus et Sanguis fiat dilectissimi Filii tui, Domini nostri Jesu Christi.*

Qui pridie quam pateretur, accepit panem in sanctas ac venerabiles manus suas, et elevatis oculis in caelum ad te Deum, Patrem suum omnipotentem, tibi gratias agens, benedixit, fregit, deditque discipulis suis, dicens: Accipite, et manducate ex hoc omnes:
HOC EST ENIM CORPUS MEUM.

Simili modo postquam coenatum est, accipiens et hunc praeclarum Calicem in sanctas ac venerabiles manus suas: item tibi gratias agens, benedixit, deditque discipulis suis, dicens: Accipite, et bibite ex eo omnes.
HOC EST ENIM CALIX SANGUINIS MEI, NOVI ET AETERNI TESTA-
MENTI
:MYSTERIUM FIDEI:
QUI PRO VOBIS ET PRO MULTIS EFFUNDETUR IN REMISSIONEM
PECCATORUM.
Haec quotiescumque feceritis, in mei memoriam facietis.

Unde et memores, Domine, nos servi tui, sed et plebs tua sancta, ejusdem Christi Filii tui, Domini nostri, tam beatae passionis, necnon et ab inferis resurrectionis, sed et in caelos gloriosae ascensionis: offerimus praeclarae majestati tuae de tuis donis ac datis, hostiam puram, hostiam sanctam, hostiam immaculatam, Panem sanctum vitae aeternae, et Calicem salutis perpetuae.

Supra quae propitio ac sereno vultu respicere digneris: et accepta habere, sicuti accepta habere dignatus es munera pueri tui justi Abel, et sacrificium Patriarchae nostri Abrahae: et quod tibi obtulit summus sacerdos tuus Melchisedech, sanctum sacrificium, immaculatam hostiam.

Supplices te rogamus, omnipotens Deus: jube haec perferri per manus sancti Angeli tui in sublime altare tuum, in conspectu divinae majestatis tuae: ut quotquot ex hac altaris participatione sacrosanctum Filii tui Corpus et Sanguinem sumpserimus, omni benedictione caelesti et gratia repleamur. Per eundem Christum Dominum nostrum. Amen." Thompson, pp. 72, 74, 76.

[18] Latin: *"Pax Domini sit semper vobiscum." "Et cum spiritu tuo."* Thompson, p. 78.
[19] Thompson, pp. 78-81, 84-85. The Latin of this last quote reads: *"Corpus Domini nostri Jesu Christi custodiat animam tuam in vitam aeternam. Amen."*
[20] Ibid., pp. 86, 88.

CONCLUSION

Jesus said, "Peace be with you! As the Father has sent Me, I am sending you." And with that He breathed on them and said, "Receive the Holy Spirit. If you forgive anyone his sins, they are forgiven; if you do not forgive them, they are not forgiven." (*John 20:21-23*)

Jesus here makes ten[1] of His eleven remaining disciples apostles; that is, "sent ones." The Lord gives the authority to forgive and retain sins first to the apostles. He gives that authority on to those whom He places into the Office of the Holy Ministry. The Lord confers this office on certain men through the action of His apostles, his apostolic ministry, and His Church. While any Christian may, in an emergency, become an *ad hoc* pastor to forgive the sins of others, the authority to forgive and retain sins on behalf of the whole Church and in the name and place of the Lord is entrusted uniquely to those who have been given the apostolic Office of the Holy Ministry.[2] It is therefore seen to be no mere coincidence that when the Lord's Supper was first instituted, its celebration was entrusted to the apostles. They were the only ones the Lord chose to have with Him when He instituted His Supper (Luke 22:14). Because the Lord's Supper is "for the forgiveness of sins" (Matt. 26:28), its celebration is given to those who hold the office which is entrusted with the forgiving and retaining of sins.

Additional scriptural evidence connecting the celebration of the Lord's Supper with the Office of the Holy Ministry has been seen. It has been noted that there is no scriptural mandate or precedent for a lay-celebration of the Lord's Supper. A lay-celebration is not from the apostles, and therefore cannot be from the Lord (1 Cor. 11:23). What is not from the Lord, the Church does not receive. She receives no novelties, nothing "beyond Christ." Rather, the Church recognizes as reliable only those celebrations of the Lord's Supper where a holder of the Office of the Holy Ministry is the celebrant.

The Office of the Holy Ministry is not, scripturally speaking, a "rank" within the Church catholic. Rather, the Lord gives the Holy Spirit to those whom He entrusts with this office for the purpose of doing all that is given to the holders of this office to do, particularly the forgiving and retaining of sins. It was noted on the preceding page that the celebrating of the Lord's Supper is a specific means of dispensing the forgiveness of sins. Therefore, one concludes that the celebration of the Lord's Supper is to be done only by one into whom the Holy Spirit has been given for this purpose.

Following the New Testament, in the earliest evidence, this exclusive connection of the Office of the Holy Ministry and the celebration of the Lord's Supper is confessed in the writings of church fathers. The reliability of the Lord's Supper was, according to Ignatius, dependent upon the connection of its celebration with the Office of the Holy Ministry. So also Clement confessed that it is as the Lord's institutions are followed that they "cannot go wrong."

In all of the foregoing there was never a mention of any such thing as a lay-celebration. Whenever a celebrant is mentioned, it is either stated or taken for granted that this celebrant will be in the Office of the Holy Ministry; that is, either a bishop or a presbyter. Of particular importance is the bestowal of the Spirit upon the ordinand in the ordination prayer of Hippolytus' *Apostolic Tradition*. The congregational response to the minister's salutation in the communion preface with the words "And with your spirit" endures to this day as a confession of the relation of the Office of the Holy Ministry to the celebration of the Lord's Supper. Without exaggeration, one may say that this was also the universal and unanimous liturgical confession of the Church.

One may have noted several apparently non-apostolic novelties which developed over the course of time. The strictly *iure humano* distinction between bishops and presbyters appears at times to be treated as though it were *iure divino*. The pure dominical gift of the Lord's Supper is sometimes treated as though it were in part, at least, the sacrificial work of man. Through it all, however, the confession that the Lord gives the forgiveness of sins to those who received His Supper was never lost. Because it was His means of forgiving sins, the confession also remained constant that the mortal instrument through which Christ celebrated was to be one into whom Christ had given the Holy Spirit for the purpose of forgiving and retaining of sins.

By the very name "the Lord's Supper," one confesses that the Supper belongs to the Lord. When a person or a group of people seeks to take it over and conform it to the traditions of men, it becomes doubtful whether or not it is still the Lord's. The Lord uses as His mouthpiece in the celebration of His Supper him upon whom He has bestowed the Spirit for the forgiving and retaining of sins. Where one into whom the Lord has not put the Spirit for this purpose attempts to celebrate, the communicant cannot be certain of what is received, whether or not the body and blood of Christ have been distributed, and whether or not the forgive-

ness of sins has been bestowed. That which is distributed
is christologically uncertain, pneumatically uncertain, and,
therefore, soteriologically uncertain.

The forgiveness of sins which the Lord offers in His Supper cannot be left uncertain. The assurance "maybe your
are forgiven" is, in fact, no assurance at all. The Lord has
entrusted the celebration of His Supper to those who are
in the Office of the Holy Ministry. Where the institution
of the Lord as it has been handed down by the apostles is
followed, there the communicant may be sure that the Lord
Himself has spoken to him, causing the bread and wine to
be His own body and blood, promising him the forgiveness
of sins and all good things that come with that forgiveness.

> What is the benefit of such eating and drinking?
> That is shown to us by these words, "Given and
> shed for you for the remission of sins"; namely, that in
> the Sacrament forgiveness of sins, life, and salvation
> are given us through these words. For where there is
> forgiveness of sins, there is also life and salvation.[3]

> But why speak I of priests? Neither Angel nor Archan-
> gel can do anything with regard to what is given from
> God; but the Father, the Son, and the Holy Ghost,
> dispenseth all, while the priest lends his tongue and
> affords his hand. For neither would it be just that
> through the wickedness of another, those who come
> in faith to the symbols of their salvation should be
> harmed. Knowing all these things, let us fear God, and
> hold His priests in honor, paying them all reverence;
> that both for our own good deeds, and the attention
> shown to them, we may receive a great return from
> God, through the grace and lovingkindness of our

Lord Jesus Christ, with whom to the Father and the
Holy Ghost be glory, dominion, and honor, now and
ever, and world without end. Amen[4]

Soli Deo Gloria

Notes:

[1] Judas had hung himself, and Thomas was not present on this occasion.
The Lord deals with Thomas specifically in the ensuing verses of the Gospel
according to St. John.

[2] There is early evidence of lay baptism and absolution in an emergency,
when a person was about to die. Never is there evidence of an emergency
that authorizes a layman to celebrate the Lord's Supper. Tr 67-68, BKS,
p. 491. Even when such an "emergency baptism" became necessary, it
was questionable whether or not it could be done by a woman. Georg
Kretschmar comments: "Nur so ist es zu verstehen, daß die Kirche, seit
dem zweiten Jahrhundert nachweisbar, also wohl seit dem Aufkommen
einer festen Taufzeit und der Ausbildung des Katechumenates, bestimmte
Möglichkeiten der Nottaufe herausstellte. Wir sind schon mehrfach darauf
gestoßen. Tertullian schreibt, daß in Notfällen, bedingt durch Ort, Zeit,
Person des Bewerbs, auch ein Laie — allerdings keine Frau — nicht nur
taufen dürfte, sondern zu taufen hätte; denn ,schuldig würde er am Verderben
eines Menschen, wenn er es unterließe das zu gewähren, was er frei geben könnte'." Georg
Kretschmar, Die Geschichte des Taufgottesdienstes in der alten Kirche. Karl Ferdinand
Müller and Walter Blankenburg, eds., Leiturgia (Kassel: Johannes Stauda
Verlag, 1970), vol. 5, p. 141.

[3] SC vi.5-6. Luther, Small Catechism, p. 21. BKS, p. 520.

[4] John Chrysostom, Homilies on St. John LXXXVI.4, NPNF 1, 14:326-327.
For the Greek, see Joannis Chrysostomi, In Joannem Homilia LXXXVI.4,
MPG, vol. 59, cols. 472-474.

APPENDIX I

Because of the critical importance of the Αποστο–
λικη παραδοσις of Hippolytus to the future development
of the liturgy, sections I.2-4a are given here according to
the Latin version. Section I.3 is also available in the Greek
Epitome of the Apostolic Constitutions. It is given in Appendix 2.

I.2 *Episcopus ordinetur electus ab omni populo, quique
cum nominatus fuerit at placuerit omnibus, conueniet populum
una cum praesbyterio et his qui praesentes fuerint episcopi, die
dominica. Consentientibus omnibus, inponant super eum manus,
et praesbyterium adstet quiescens. Omnes autem silentium habeant,
orantes in corde propter discensionem spiritus. Ex quibus unus de
praesentibus episcopis, ab omnibus rogatus, inponens manum ei qui
ordinatur episcopus, oret ita dicens :*

I.3 *Deus et pater domini nostri Iesu Christi, pater mi-
sericordiarum et deus totius consolationis, qui in excelsis habitas et
humilia respices, qui cognoscis omnia antequam nascantur, tu qui
dedisti terminos in ecclesia per uerbum gratiae tuae, praedestinans
ex principio genus iustorum Abraham, principes et sacerdotes con-
stituens, et sanctum tuum sine ministerio non derelinquens, ex initio
saeculi bene tibi placuit in his quos elegisti dari : nunc effunde eam
uirtutem, quae a te est, principalis spiritus, quem dedisti dilecto filio
tuo Iesu Christo, quod donauit sanctis apostolis, qui constituerunt
ecclesiam per singula loca sanctifictionem tuam, in gloriam et laudem
indeficientem no mini tuo.*

*Da, cordis cognitor pater, super hunc seruum tuum, quem
elegisti ad episcopatum, pascere gregem sanctam tuam, et primatum
sacerdotii tibi exhibere sine repraehensione, seruientem noctu et die,*

incessanter repropitiari uultum tuum et offerre dona sanctae ecclesiae tuae, spiritum primatus sacerdotii habere potestatem dimittere peccata secundum mandatum tuum, dare sortes secundum praeceptum tuum, soluere etiam omnem collegationem secundum potestatem quam dedisti apostolis, placere autem tibi in mansuetudine et mundo corde, offerentem tibi odorem suauitatis, per peurum tuum Iesum Christum, per quem tibi gloria et potentia et honor, patri et filio cum spiritu sancto et nunc et in saecula saeculorum. Amen.

I.4 *Qui cumque factus fuerit episcopus, omnes os offerant pacis, salutantes eum quia dignus effectus est. Illi uero offerant diacones oblationes, quique inponens manus in eum cum omni praesbyterio dicat gratians agens :*

Dominus uobiscum.

Et omnes dicant :

Et cum spiritu tuo.

Sursum corda.

Habemus ad dominum.

Gratias agamus domino.

Dignum et iustum est.

Et sic iam prosequatur :

(The prayer of consecration of the elements of the Lord's Supper follows here, and it includes the dominical words of institution.)

Botte, <u>Sources</u> 11:40, 42, 44, 46, 48.

APPENDIX II

The Greek text of the ordination prayer of the Αποστολικη παραδοσις (I.3) is taken from the Epitome of the Apostolic Constitutions, and reads as follows:

I.3 Ο Θεος και πατιρ του κυριου ημων Ιησου Χριστου, ο πατηρ των οικτριμων και Θεος πασης παρακλησεως, ο εν υψηλοις κατοικων και τα ταπεινα εφορων, ο γινωσκων τα παντα πριν γενεσεως αυτων, συ ο δους ορους εκκλησιας δια λογου χαριτος σου, ο προοριας τε απ αρχης γενος δικαιον εξ Αβρααμ, αρχοντας τε και ιερεις καταστησας, το τε αγιασμα σου μη καταλιπων αλειτουργητον, ο απο καταβολης χοσμου ευδοκησας εν οις ηρετισω δοξασθηναι: και νυν επιχεε την παρα σου δυναμιν του ηγεμονικου πνευματος, οπερ δια του ηγαπημενου σου παιδος Ιησου Χριστου δεδωρησαι τοις αγιοις σου αποστολοις, οι καθιδρυσαν την εκκλησιαν κατα τοπον αγιασματος σου εις δοξαν και αινον αδιαλειπτον του ονοματος σου. Καρδιογνωστα παντων δος επι τον δουλον σου τουτον ον εξ ελεξω εις επισκοπην [ποιμαινεν την ποιμνην] σου την αγιαν, και αρχιερατευειν σοι αμεμπτως, λειτουργουντα ψυκτος και ημερας, αδιαλειπτως τε ιλασκεσθαι τω προσωπω σου και προσφερειν σοι τα δωρα της αγιας σου εκκλησιας, και τω πνευματι τω αρχιερατικω εκειν εξουσιαν αφιεναι αμαρτιας κατα την εφντολην σου, διδοναι κληρους κατα το προσταγμα σου, λυειν τε παντα συνδεσμον κατα την εξουσιαν η εδωκας τοις αποστολοις, ευαρεστειν τε σοι εν πραοτητι και καθαρα καρδια, προσφεροντα σοι οσμην ευωδιας δια του παιδος σου Ιησου Χριστου του κυριου ημων, μεθ ου σοι δοξα, κρατος, τιμη, συν αγιω πνευματι, νυν και αει και εις

τους αιωνας των αιωνων. Αμην.
Botte, <u>Sources</u> 11:42, 44, 46.

BIBLIOGRAPHY

Primary Sources

Ambrose, *De Sacramentis*. Translated by Roy J. Deferrari. The Fathers of the Church. Volume 44. Washington, D. C.: The Catholic University of America Press, 1963.

Ambrose, *De Sacramentis*. Edited by Bernard Botte. Sources Chrétiennes. Volume 25. Paris: Les Éditions du Cerf, 1961.

The Anaphora of Addai and Mari. Translated in Lucien Deiss. Springtime of the Liturgy. Translated by Matthew J. O'Connell. Collegeville, MN: The Liturgical Press, 1979.

Anaphora Iacobi Fratris Domini. Edited by Anton Hänggi and Irmgard Pahl. Prex Eucharistica. Fribourg, Switzerland: Éditions Universitaires Fribourg Suisse, 1968.

Anaphora Ioannis Chrysostomi. Edited by Anton Hänggi and Irmgard Pahl. Prex Eucharistica. Fribourg, Switzerland: Éditions Universitaires Fribourg Suisse, 1968.

Anaphora Marci Evangelistae. Edited by Anton Hänggi and Irmgard Pahl. Prex Eucharistica. Fribourg, Switzerland: Éditions Universitaires Fribourg Suisse, 1968.

Canons of the 150 Fathers who Assembled at Constantinople. Edited by Henry R. Percival. Philip Schaff and Henry Wace, gen. eds. Nicene and Post-Nicene Fathers. Series 2, Volume 14. Grand Rapids, MI: Wm. B. Eerdmans Publishing Company, 1988.

The Canons of the 318 Holy Fathers Assembled in the City of Nice, in

190

Bithynia. Edited by Henry R. Percival. Philip Schaff and Henry Wace, gen. eds. Nicene and Post-Nicene Fathers. Series 2, Volume 14. Grand Rapids, MI: Wm. B. Eerdmans Publishing Company, 1988.

Clement of Rome. *Corinthians*. Edited by J. B. Lightfoot and J. R. Harmer. The Apostolic Fathers. Grand Rapids, MI: Baker Book House, 1988.

Concelebratio Eucharistica Ritu Hispano Veteri Seu Mozarabico. Salamanca, Spain: Calatrava, 1976.

Concilium Chalcedonese, Canones. Conciliorum Oecumenicorum Decreta. Bologna, Italy: Instituto per le Scienze Religiose, 1972.

Concilium Constantinopolitanum I, Canones. Conciliorum Oecumenicorum Decreta. Bologna, Italy: Instituto per le Scienze Religiose, 1972.

Concilium Nicaenum I, Canones. Conciliorum Oecumenicorum Decreta. Bologna, Italy: Instituto per le Scienze Religiose, 1972.

Les Constitutions Apostoliques. Three Volumes. Edited by Marcel Metzger. Sources Chretiennes. Volumes 320, 329, 336. Paris: Les Editions du Cerf, 1985-1987.

Constitutions of the Holy Apostles. Edited by Alexander Roberts and James Donaldson. The Ante-Nicene Fathers. Volume 7. Grand Rapids, MI: Wm. B. Eerdmans Publishing Company, 1985.

Cyril of Jerusalem. *Mystagogical Catecheses*. Edited by F. L. Cross. St. Cyril of Jerusalem's Lectures on the Christian Sacraments. London: SPCK, 1951.

Deiss, Lucien. Springtime of the Liturgy. Translated by Matthew J. O'Connell. Collegeville, MN: The Liturgical Press, 1979.

Didache. Jurgens, William A. The Faith of the Early Fathers. Volume 1. Collegeville, MN: The Liturgical Press, 1970.

Didache. Edited by J. B. Lightfoot and J. R. Harmer. The Apostolic Fathers. Grand Rapids, MI: Baker Book House, 1988.

Didascalia Apostolorum. Translated from the Syriac, and accompanied by the Verona Latin Fragments, by R. Hugh Connolly. London: Oxford University Press, 1929.

The *Didascalia Apostolorum* in English. Translated from the Syriac by Margaret Dunlop Gibson. London: Cambridge University Press, 1903.

The *Didascalia Apostolorum* in Syriac, Chapters I-X. Tome 176. Translated by Arthur Vööbus. Louvain, Belgium: Corpus Scriptorum Christianorum Orientalum, 1979.

The *Didascalia Apostolorum* in Syriac, Chapters I-X. Tome 175. Edited by Arthur Vööbus. Louvain, Belgium: Corpus Scriptorum Christianorum Orientalum, 1979.

The *Didascalia Apostolorum* in Syriac, Chapters XI-XXVI. Tome 179. Edited by Arthur Vööbus. Louvain, Belgium: Corpus Scriptorum Christianorum Orientalum, 1979.

The Divine Liturgy of James, the Holy Apostle and Brother of the Lord. Edited by Alexander Roberts and James Donaldson. The Ante-Nicene Fathers. Volume 7. Grand Rapids, MI: Wm. B. Eerdmans Publishing Company, 1985.

The Divine Liturgy of Saint John Chrysostom. Translated by the Faculty of Hellenic College/Holy Cross Greek Orthodox School of Theology. Brookline, MA: Holy Cross Orthodox Press, 1985.

Hippolyte de Rome. *La Tradition Apostolique*. Edited by Bernard Botte. Sources Chretiennes. Volume 11. Paris, Les Editions du Cerf, 1968.

Hippolytus. The Apostolic Tradition. Translated and edited by Burton Scott Easton. Cambridge University Press, 1934.

_____. *Refutation of All Heresies*. Edited by Alexander Roberts and James Donaldson. The Ante-Nicene Fathers. Volume 5. Grand Rapids, MI: Wm. B. Eerdmans Publishing Company, 1985.

_____. Refutatio Omnium Haeresium. Edited by Miroslav Marcovich. Berlin: Walter de Gruyter, 1986.

The Holy Bible, New International Version. Copyright International Bible Society, 1973, 1978, 1984. Used by permission of Zondervan Bible Publishers.

The Holy Bible, Revised Standard Version. Grand Rapids, MI: Zondervan Publishing House, 1952.

Ignatius. *Ephesians*. Edited by J. B. Lightfoot and J. R. Harmer. The Apostolic Fathers. Grand Rapids, MI: Baker Book House, 1988.

_____. *Magnesians*. Edited by J. B. Lightfoot and J. R. Harmer. The Apostolic Fathers. Grand Rapids, MI: Baker Book House, 1988.

_____. *Trallians*. Edited by J. B. Lightfoot and J. R. Harmer. The Apostolic Fathers. Grand Rapids, MI: Baker Book House, 1988.

_____. *Philadelphians*. Edited by J. B. Lightfoot and J. R.

Harmer. The Apostolic Fathers. Grand Rapids, MI: Baker Book House, 1988.

_____. *To Polycarp.* Edited by J. B. Lightfoot and J. R. Harmer. The Apostolic Fathers. Grand Rapids, MI: Baker Book House, 1988.

_____. *Smyrnæans.* Edited by J. B. Lightfoot and J. R. Harmer. The Apostolic Fathers. Grand Rapids, MI: Baker Book House, 1988.

Joannis Chrysostomi. *In Joannem Homilia* LXXXXVI. Edited by J. P. Migne. Patrologiæ Series Græca. Volume 59, columns 467-474. Paris, 1857-1866.

John Chrysostom. *Homilies on St. John* LXXXVI. Philip Schaff and Henry Wace, gen. eds. Nicene and Post-Nicene Fathers. Series 1. Volume 14. Grand Rapids, MI: Wm. B. Eerdmans Publishing Company, 1988.

Justin Martyr. *First Apology.* Translated by Marcus Dods. Edited by Alexander Roberts and James Donaldson. Ante-Nicene Christian Library. Volume 2. Edinburgh: T. and T. Clark, 1867.

_____. *First Apology.* Edited by J. P. Migne. Patrologiæ Series Græca. Volume 6, columns 327-440. Paris, 1857-1866.

_____. *Dialogue with Trypho.* Translated by G. Reith. Edited by Alexander Roberts and James Donaldson. Ante-Nicene Christian Library. Volume 2. Edinburgh: T. and T. Clark, 1867.

_____. *Dialogue with Trypho.* Edited by J. P. Migne. Patrologiæ Series Græca. Volume 6, columns 471-800. Paris, 1857-1866.

Le Liber Mozarabicus Sacramentorum et les Manuscrits Mozarabes.

Edited by D. Marius Férotin. Monumenta Ecclesiae Liturgica. Volume 6. Paris: Librairie de Firmin-Didot, 1912.

Le Liber Ordinum en Usage Dans l'Eglise Wisigothique et Mozarabe d'Espagne. Edited by D. Marius Férotin. Monumenta Ecclesiae Liturgica. Volume 5. Paris: Librairie de Firmin-Didot, 1904.

Liturgia Mozarabica. Edited by J. P. Migne. Patrologiæ, Series Latina. Volume 85. Paris, 1862.

The Liturgies of S. Basil and S. Chrysostom. Translated by F. E. Brightman. Liturgies Eastern and Western. Volume 1: Eastern Liturgies. London: Henry Frowde, 1896.

The Liturgy of the Coptic Jacobites. Translated by F. E. Brightman. Liturgies Eastern and Western. Volume 1: Eastern Liturgies. London: Henry Frowde, 1896.

The Liturgy of the Nestorians including The Anaphora of Ss. Addai and Mari. Translated by F. E. Brightman. Liturgies Eastern and Western. Volume 1: Eastern Liturgies. London: Henry Frowde, 1896.

The Liturgy of Saint James. Translated by F. E. Brightman. Liturgies Eastern and Western. Volume 1: Eastern Liturgies. London: Henry Frowde, 1896.

The Liturgy of Saint James. Edited by R. C. D. Jasper and G. J. Cuming. Prayers of the Eucharist. New York: Pueblo Publishing Company, 1987.

The Liturgy of Saint John Chrysostom. Edited by R. C. D. Jasper and G. J. Cuming. Prayers of the Eucharist. New York: Pueblo Publishing Company, 1987.

The Liturgy of Saint Mark. Translated by F. E. Brightman. Liturgies Eastern and Western. Volume 1: Eastern Liturgies. London: Henry Frowde, 1896.

The Liturgy of Saint Mark. Edited by R. C. D. Jasper and G. J. Cuming. Prayers of the Eucharist. New York: Pueblo Publishing Company, 1987.

The Liturgy of Saints Addai and Mari. Edited by R. C. D. Jasper and G. J. Cuming. Prayers of the Eucharist. New York: Pueblo Publishing Company, 1987.

The Liturgy of the Syrian Jacobites. Translated by F. E. Brightman. Liturgies Eastern and Western. Volume 1: Eastern Liturgies. London: Henry Frowde, 1896.

Lutheran Book of Worship. Minneapolis, MN: Augsburg Publishing House, 1978.

Lutheran Worship. St. Louis, MO: Concordia Publishing House, 1982.

Macomber, William F. "The Oldest Known Text of the Anaphora of the Apostles [Addai and Mari]." Orientala Christiana Periodica 32 (1966):335-371.

The Mass of the Roman Rite. Edited by R. C. D. Jasper and G. J. Cuming. Prayers of the Eucharist. New York: Pueblo Publishing Company, 1987.

The Mozarabic Rite. Edited by R. C. D. Jasper and G. J. Cuming. Prayers of the Eucharist. New York: Pueblo Publishing Company, 1987.

The Mar Thoma Syrian Liturgy. Translated by George Kuttickal

Chacko. New York: Morehouse-Gorham Co., 1956.

Narsai, *An Exposition of the Mysteries (Hom. XVII)*. Edited by R. H. Connolly. The Liturgical Homilies of Narsai. London: Cambridge University Press, 1909.

Narsai, Homiliæ et Carmina. Edited by D. Alphonsi Mingana. Volume 1. Mausilii: Typis Fratrum Prædicatorum, 1905.

Novum Testamentum Graece et Latine. Edited by Eberhard Nestle, Erwin Nestle, and Kurt Aland. Stuttgart: Deutsche Bibelgesellschaft, 1984.

The Order of Low Mass. Bard Thompson. The Liturgies of the Western Church. Philadelphia: Fortress Press, 1985. Pages 54-91. "Transcribed from *The Missal in Latin and English*, being the text of the *Missale Romanum* with English rubrics and a new translation (Westminster: Newman Press, 1959), pp. 676-720."

Ordo Antiquus Gallicanus. Edited by Klaus Gamber. Regensburg: Verlag Friedrich Pustet, 1965.

St. Cyril of Jerusalem's Lectures on the Christian Sacraments. Edited by F. L. Cross. London: SPCK, 1951.

Die Syrische Jakobosanaphora. Edited by Adolf Rücker. Münster in Westfalen, Germany: Verlag der Aschendorffschen Verlagsbuchhandlung, 1923.

The XXX Canons of the Holy and Fourth Synod's, of Chalcedon. Edited by Henry R. Percival. Philip Schaff and Henry Wace, gen. eds. Nicene and Post-Nicene Fathers. Series 2, Volume 14. Grand Rapids, MI: Wm. B. Eerdmans Publishing Company, 1988.

Secondary Sources

Aalen, Sverre. "Das Abendmahl als Opfermahl bei Paulus." Novum Tesamentum 6 (1963):128-152.

Bailey, Henry I. The Liturgy Compared with the Bible. London: S.P.C.K., 1845.

Barnes, Albert. Notes on the Epistle to the Hebrews. Revised Edition. London: George Routledge and Sons, n.d.

Baldovin, John F. Liturgy in Ancient Jerusalem. Bramcote, GB: Grove Books, 1989.

Bauer, Walter. A Greek-English Lexicon of the New Testament and Other Early Christian Literature. Translated by William F. Arndt and F. Wilbur Gingrich. Revised by F. Wilbur Gingrich and Frederick W. Danker. Chicago: University of Chicago Press, 1979.

Die Bekenntnisschriften der evangelisch=lutherischen Kirche. Göttingen: Vanderhoeck & Ruprecht, 1986.

Bishop, Edmund. "On the Early Texts of the Roman Canon." Journal of Theological Studies 4 (1903):555-577.

Bishop, W. C. "The African Rite." Journal of Theological Studies 13 (1911-1912):250-277.

_____. The Mozarabic and Ambrosian Rites. Edited by C. L. Feltoe. Milwaukee: The Morehouse Publishing Co., 1924.

Bläser, Peter; Suso Frank; Peter Manns; Gerhard Fahrnberger; and Hans-Joachim Schulz. Amt und Eucharistie. Paderborn: Verlag Bonifacius-Druckerei, 1973.

Blond, Georges. *Clement of Rome*. The Eucharist of the Early Christians. Translated by Matthew J. O'Connell. New York: Pueblo Publishing Company, 1978. Pages 24-47.

The Book of Concord. Edited by Theodore G. Tappert. Philadelphia: Fortress Press, 1959.

Bouyer, Louis. Eucharist. Translated by Charles Underhill Quinn. Notre Dame, IN: University of Notre Dame Press, 1968.

Bradshaw, Paul F. Ordination Rites of the Ancient Churches. New York: Pueblo Publishing Company, 1990.

Brightman, F. E. Liturgies Eastern and Western. Volume 1: Eastern Liturgies. London: Henry Frowde, 1896.

Brown, Francis; S. R. Driver and Charles A. Briggs. Hebrew and English Lexicon. Peabody, MA: Hendrickson Publishers, 1979.

Cabié, Robert. *The Eucharist*. Translated by Matthew J. O'Connell. Edited by A. G. Martimort. The Church at Prayer, new edition. Volume 2. Collegeville, MD: The Liturgical Press, 1986.

Chytraeus, David. On Sacrifice. Translated by John Warwick Montgomery. St. Louis, MO: Concordia Publishing House, 1962.

Connolly, R. H., ed. *Didascalia Apostolorum*. London: Oxford University Press, 1929.

_____. The Liturgical Homilies of Narsai. London: Cambridge University Press, 1909.

Cuming, G. J. "The Anaphora of St. Mark: A Study in Development." Le Muséon 95 (1982):115-129.

Dallmann, William. The Real Presence. Pittsburgh, PA: American Lutheran Publication Board, 1900.

Daniel, K. N. A Critical Study of Primitive Liturgies. Kottayam, India: C. M. S. Press, 1937.

Deiss, Lucien. Springtime of the Liturgy. Translated by Matthew J. O'Connell. Collegeville, MN: The Liturgical Press, 1979.

Denis-Boulet, Noèle Maurice and Roger Béraudy. The Church at Prayer. Volume 2: *The Eucharist*. Edited by A. G. Martimort. Translated by Daniel Farrelly. New York: Herder and Herder, 1973.

Dix, Gregory. The Shape of the Liturgy. London: Dacre Press, 1960.

Elert, Werner. The Lord's Supper Today. Translated by Martin Bertram and Rudolph F. Norden. St. Louis, MO: Concordia Publishing House, 1973.

Empie, Paul C., and T. Austin Murphy, eds. *Eucharist & Ministry*. Lutherans and Catholics in Dialogue. Volume 4. Minneapolis, MN: Augsburg Publishing House, 1979.

Funk, F. X., ed. Didascalia et Constitutiones Apostolorum. Torino, Italy: Bogetta d'Erasmo, 1959.

Guthrie, Donald. New Testament Theology. Downers Grove, IL: Inter-Varsity Press, 1981.
Hammond, Charles E. Liturgies Eastern and Western. London: Oxford University Press, 1878.

Hänggi, Anton; and Irmgard Pahl. Prex Eucharistica. Fribourg, Switzerland: Éditions Universitaires Fribourg Suisse, 1968.

Harris, R. Laird. Theological Wordbook of the Old Testament. 2 Volumes. Chicago: The Moody Bible Institute, 1980.

Hein, Kenneth. Eucharist and Excommunication. Bern: Herbert Lang & Co., 1973.

Holwerda, David Earl. The Holy Spirit and Eschatology in the Gospel of John. Kampen: J. H. Kok N. V., 1959.

Hummel, Horace D. The Word Becoming Flesh. St. Louis, MO: Concordia Publishing House, 1979.

The Inspiration of Scripture. A Report of the Commission on Theology and Church Relations, The Lutheran Church-Missouri Synod, March 1975.

Jasper, R. C. D. and Cuming, G. J. Prayers of the Eucharist, Early and reformed. Third Revised Edition. New York: Pueblo Publishing Company, 1980.

Jeremias, Joachim. The Eucharistic Words of Jesus. Translated by Norman Perrin. Philadelphia: Fortress Press, 1986.

Johanny, Raymond. *Ignatius of Antioch*. The Eucharist of the Early Christians. Translated by Matthew J. O'Connell. New York: Pueblo Publishing Company, 1978. Pages 48-70.

Jones, Cheslyn; Geoffrey Wainwright; and Edward Yarnold, eds. The Study of the Liturgy. New York: Oxford University Press, 1978.

Jourjon, Maurice. *Justin*. The Eucharist of the Early Christians. Translated by Matthew J. O'Connell. New York: Pueblo Publishing Company, 1978. Pages 71-85.

Jungmann, Joseph A. The Mass of the Roman Rite: Its Origins and Development. 2 Volumes. Translated by Francis A. Brunner. New York: Benziger Brothers, 1951.

Jurgens, William A. The Faith of the Early Fathers. Volume 1. Collegeville, MN: The Liturgical Press, 1970.

Keifer, Ralph A. "The Unity of the Roman Canon: An Examination of its Unique Structure." Studia Liturgica 11 (1976):39.

Keil, C. F., and F. Delitzsch. Commentary on the Old Testament. 10 Volumes. Grand Rapids, MI: William B. Eerdmans Publishing Co., 1985.

Kilmartin, Edward J. "Ministry and Ordination in Early Christianity against a Jewish Background." Studia Liturgica 13 (1979):42-69.

King, Archdale A. Liturgies of the Primatial Sees. Milwaukee: The Bruce Publishing Company, 1957.

Kittel, Gerhard, ed. Theological Dictionary of the New Testament. 10 Volumes. Translated by Geoffrey W. Bromiley. Grand Rapids, MI: Wm B. Eerdmans Publishing Company, 1987.

Klauser, Theodor. A Short History of the Western Liturgy. Translated by John Halliburton. London: Oxford University Press, 1969.

Kretschmar, Georg. "Die Geschichte des Taufgottesdienstes in der alten Kirche." Edited by Karl Ferdinand Müller and Walter Blankenburg. Leiturgia. Kassel: Johannes Stauda Verlag, 1954. Volume 5, pages 1-346.

Lenski, R. C. H. The Interpretation of St. Paul's First and Second Epistles to the Corinthians. Minneapolis, MN: Augsburg

Publishing House, 1963.

Lietzmann, Hans. Mass And Lord's Supper. Translated by Dorothea H. G. Reeve. Introduction and Further Inquiry by Robert Douglas Richardson. Leiden, Netherlands: E. J. Brill, 1979.

Lietzmann, Hans. Messe und Herrenmahl. Bonn: A. Marcus und E. Weber's Verlag, 1926.

Lohse, Eduard. Die Ordination im Spätjudentum und im Neuen Testament. Göttingen: Vanderhoeck & Ruprecht, 1951.

Luther, Martin. Small Catechism, revised edition. St. Louis, MO: Concordia Publishing House, 1965.

Macomber, William F. "The Oldest Known Text of the Anaphora of the Apostles [Addai and Mari]." Orientala Christiana Periodica 32 (1966):335-371.

Metzger, Marcel. The Didascalia and the Constitutiones Apostolorum. The Eucharist of the Early Christians. Translated by Matthew J. O'Connell. New York: Pueblo Publishing Company, 1978. Pages 194-219.

Murphy, John L. The Mass and Liturgical Reform. Milwaukee: The Bruce Publishing Company, 1956.

Pieper, Francis. Christian Dogmatics. 3 Volumes. St. Louis, MO: Concordia Publishing House, 1950.

Pieper, Franz. Christliche Dogmatik. 3 Volumes. St. Louis, MO: Concordia Publishing House, 1924.

Porter, William S. The Gallican Rite. London: A. R. Mowbray & Co., 1958.

Preus, Robert. The Inspiration of Scripture. Second edition. London: Oliver and Boyd, 1957.

Quasten, Johannes. Patrology. Volume 1. Westminster, MD: The Newman Press, 1951.

Quecke, H. "Ein säidischer Zeuge der Markusliturgie (Brit. Mus. Nr. 54036)." Orientalia Christiana Periodica 37 (1971):40-54.

Ratcliff, Edward C. "The Original Form of the Anaphora of Addai and Mari: A Suggestion." The Journal of Theological Studies 30 (1929):23-32.

Rordorf, Willy. The Didache. The Eucharist of the Early Christians. Translated by Matthew J. O'Connell. New York: Pueblo Publishing Company, 1978.

Sasse, Hermann. We Confess the Sacraments. Translated by Norman Nagel. St. Louis, MO: Concordia Publishing House, 1985.

Scaer, David. Ordination: Human Rite or Divine Ordinance? Fort Wayne, IN: Concordia Theological Seminary Press, n.d.

Schmemann, Alexander. Introduction to Liturgical Theology. Translated by Asheleigh E. Moorehouse. New York: St. Vladimir's Seminary Press, 1986.

Schrieber, Paul L. "Priests Among Priests: The Office of the Ministry in Light of the Old Testament Priesthood." Concordia Journal 14 (July 1988):215-228.

Schulz, Hans-Joachim. The Byzantine Liturgy. Translated by Matthew J. O'Connell. New York: Pueblo Publishing Company, 1986.

Shepherd Jr., Massey H. "Eusebius and the Liturgy of Saint James." Yearbook of Liturgical Studies. Volume 4. Notre Dame, IN: Fides Publishers, 1963. Pages 109-123.

Spinks, Bryan D. Addai and Mari—the Anaphora of the Apostles: A Text for Students. Bramcote, GB: Grove Books, 1980.

_____. "A Complete Anaphora? A Note on Strasbourg Gr.254." The Heythrop Journal 25 (1984):51-55.

_____. "The Consecratory Epiklesis in the Anaphora of St. James." Studia Liturgica 11 (1976):19-38.

Stählin, Rudolph. "Die Geschichte des christlichen Gottesdienstes von der Urkirche bis zur Gaegenwart." Edited by Karl Ferdinand Müller and Walter Blankenburg. Leiturgia. Volume 1, pages 1-80. Kassel: Johannes Stauda Verlag, 1954.

Stam, John E. Episcopacy in the Apostolic Tradition of Hippolytus. Basel: Friedrich Reinhardt Kommissionsverlag, 1969.

A Statement of Scriptural and Confessional Principles. Adopted by The Lutheran Church-Missouri Synod, 50th Regular Convention, July 6-13, 1973; Resolution 3-01, *Proceedings*, pages 127-128. Reprinted by the Commission on Theology and Church Relations, n.d.

Stevenson, Kenneth. "Eucharistic Offering: Does Research into Origins make any Difference?" Studia Liturgica 15 (1982/1983):87-103.

Strittmatter, Anselm. "'Missa Grecorum.' 'Missa Sancti Iohannis Crisostomi.' The Oldest Latin Version Known of the Byzantine Liturgies of St. Basil and St. John Chrysostom." Traditio 1 (1943):79-137.

Thompson, Bard. Liturgies of the Western Church. Philadelphia: Fortress Press, 1961.

Van Unnik, W. C. *Dominus Vobiscum*. New Testament Essays: Studies in Memory of Thomas Walter Manson. Edited by A. J. B. Higgins. Manchester, GB: University of Manchester Press, 1959. Pages 270-305.

Vööbus, Arthur. History of the School of Nisibis. Louvain: Corpus Scriptorum Christianorum Orientalum, 1965.

Wagner, Georg. Der Ursprung der Chrysostomusliturgie. Aschendorff, Münster Westfalen, Germany: Aschendorffsche Buchdruckerei, 1973.

Walther, C. F. W. Church and Ministry. Translated by J. T. Mueller. St. Louis, MO: Concordia Publishing House, 1987.

Ware, Timothy. The Orthodox Church. New York: Penguin Books, 1964.

Willis, Geoffrey G. Essays in Early Roman Liturgy. London: S.P.C.K., 1964.

_____. Further Essays in Early Roman Liturgy. London: S.P.C.K., 1968.